Science Actual Size

36 Complete Lesson Plans!

Sunflower
education

Exceptional Books for Teachers and Parents™

A Great Way to Teach Science!

Kids love making and interacting with these creative full-scale chalk drawings—it's the next-best thing to being there! *Actual Size—Science* makes it easy for you and your students to accurately draw life-sized dinosaurs, the world's longest snake, and other animals. You can make a scale model of the Grand Canyon and the eye of a hurricane. Draw the International Space Station and Sputnik—in actual size! Detailed lesson plans and precise blueprints guide you in creating experiences your students will never forget.

36 Complete Lesson Plans • 36 Accurate Blueprints

Please feel free to photocopy the sheets in this book within reason. Sunflower Education grants teachers permission to photocopy the activity sheets from this book for educational use. This permission is granted to individual teachers and not entire schools or school systems. Please send any permissions questions to permissions@SunflowerEducation.net.

Visit **SunflowerEducation.Net** for more great books!

Editorial	Sunflower Education
Design	Cynthia Hannon Design
Illustrations:	Miranda Mueller

Photography:
Cover image, ©Poznyakov/Shutterstock Images LLC
Interior images, Wikimedia Commons

ISBN-13: 978-1-937166-05-2
ISBN-10: 1-937166-05-8
Copyright © 2013
Sunflower Education
All rights reserved.
Printed in the U.S.A.

Table of Contents

Technology

To the Teacher

Turn the playground into a landscape for learning—and get ready to have some fun! *Actual Size—Science* brings high-interest science topics to life.

How *Actual Size—Science* is Organized

Actual Size—Science includes 36 delightful activities. Each one focuses on an actual size (full scale) or small-scale drawing or diagram of a high-interest science topic.

Each activity consist of two pages:
- The ***Activity Page*** provides teaching material for how to create and use the drawing or diagram.
- The ***Plan Page*** provides the blueprint for the drawing or diagram itself.

Materials Needed

The materials needed for each activity are listed in the Prepare section of each Activity Page. For most activities, the key tools are:

- sidewalk chalk (and lots of it!)
- a meter or yardstick
- a measuring tape and/or a measuring wheel
- a carpenter's square
- chalk line reel

A few activities require a string and stakes (for drawing circles and ellipses). Other activities that involve drawing small-scale diagrams require small-scale human figures or objects. These are included on the Plan Pages. You should plan on copying those pages and cutting them out.

How to Use this Book

You may wish to integrate these activities into your curriculum or you may wish to use them as standalone fun. Teachers have used these activities as:

- lesson/topic openers
- main lesson topics
- extension activities
- enrichment activities
- independent class rewards

To the Teacher

A general lesson cycle for using the *Actual Size—Science* includes the following steps, detailed on each of the Activity Pages:

Prepare

Each Activity Page begins with "Prepare." There are two parts to Prepare: *Allow time* is the approximate amount of time the activity will take. *Gather materials* lists the materials you will need for the activity.

Focus

Each Activity Page follows Prepare with "Focus." Focus includes bellringer and/or background information about the topic to help you get students excited about the lesson.

Present

Each Activity Page follows Focus with "Present." Present provides step-by-step instructions for creating the drawing or diagram and leading your students in interacting with it. Here is where the real learning—and the real fun!—takes place. Depending on your situation, you may wish to create the drawing or diagram yourself or, more likely, to divvy up tasks among your students working individually or in groups or as a class. *Actual Size—Science* can be used with children of all different ages; simply adjust the amount of help you give them as they draw the diagrams accordingly.

Many of the diagrams were drawn very simply so that they would be easier for children to replicate. If you wish, you can show students relevant photographs and paintings of their subject (included on the Activity Pages) to provide them with more detail. Older or more advanced students can add greater details to their illustrations. You will notice that several of the projects are very large. Depending on the space and time you have available, you may want to draw some of these diagrams or drawings at half or quarter scale.

Notice any boldfaced vocabulary terms that you may integrate into the activity. At the end of Present is a list of the vocabulary term(s) with concise definitions that you can share with your students.

KEY: Above all else, make sure that kids have the freedom to wander in and out of what they created, play (younger children enjoy make-believing), ask questions, and simply enjoy themselves. Essentially, you have just led them in creating a two-dimensional (and sometimes three-dimensional) specialized playscape. Let them have fun!

Conclude

Each Activity Page ends with "Conclude." Here you will find ways to wind the lesson down, questions for you and the students to discuss, or extension activities. They can help students concretize the ideas they encountered during the activity.

Pedagogy

The activities in *Actual Size—Science* fall under many pedagogical categories. These activities are kinesthetic, multisensory, interdisciplinary, concrete, accommodating, converging, diverging, assimilating "hands-on," project-based, grouped, and so on. Depending on your focus, and your pedagogical leanings, any of these aspects can be highlighted.

However you categorize the activities, though, the research is clear: the activities in *Actual Size—Science* are pedagogically sound. According to the U.S. Department of Education, "the use of multiple representations—pictures, diagrams, charts and models—helps students visualize and understand difficult concepts." Further, "research has found that when teachers make connections between abstract and concrete representations, students are better able to apply what they have learned across a range of situations."

But, a simpler test is this: ask an adult to recall something from their own school days. Chances are, it will be a project or an activity. *Actual Size—Science* is designed to help you create projects and lead activities that your students will find, literally, unforgettable!

We had one teacher share this about her experience: "My students got to see the fruits of their labor in just one class. It made them feel confident in themselves and in their imaginations."

Confident kids—is there anything better?

Care to share? We would love to see pictures of your students' creations.
Please email them to info@SunflowerEducation.net.

You can also learn about *Actual Size—Social Studies*,
the companion book to *Actual Size—Science*.

Visit SunflowerEducation.net

Grab some chalk
and get ready
for some fun!

Vocabulary Terms

Every activity in *Actual Size–Science* introduces students to one or more important vocabulary terms. Here they all are in one place.

Aboriginal: a member of the earliest known people of Australia

adapted: well-suited to the world around you

Arctic: the top of the Earth around the North Pole

artificial: made by people, not naturally occurring

astronomical unit (AU): the distance between the Sun and the Earth (about 93 million miles)

atmosphere: a layer of gases that surrounds the earth

baleen: rows of hard plates that hang down from the upper jaw of some whales

bathyscaphe: a ship that can travel far down into the ocean

biodiversity: variety of living things

burrow: a hole dug by a small animal and used as a place to live

canopy: the top part of the kelp

canyon: a deep valley with steep sides

carnivore: an animal that eats other animals

carrion: animals that are already dead

cloud: a mass of droplets of water or ice in the air that you can see

collide: to hit something while moving

colonize: to settle in a new place

computer: a machine, usually electronic, that can take in, store, and make calculations with information

coral reef: one of the massive underwater structures built by the remains of coral

coral: another name for polyps or their remains

crater: a hole in the ground, often created by a meteorite

data: a list of the outcomes of many experiments; information

digital: electronic

dinosaur: any member of a group of lizard-like animals varying greatly in size that roamed the Earth for 160 million years

drill: a tool that can be used to make holes in something

droplet: a tiny drop

endangered: a species threatened to go extinct, or disappear completely

evaporate: when water turns into vapor

extinct: no longer exists or lives anywhere

eye of a hurricane: the calm area at the middle of the storm

eyewall: the stormy border of the hurricane's eye

fossil fuel: fuel that is formed from the remains of plants and animals

functional: working

generate: to make something

glacier: a huge river of ice that moves over land

global warming: the gradual warming of the Earth's atmosphere caused by people

grand: big or amazing

hadron: a type of particle

herd: a group of animals living together

international: involving two or more countries

invent: to make something that is completely new

invertebrate: an animal without a backbone

iron ore: a rock or mineral in which iron can be found

krill: a small shrimp-like animal that lives in the ocean

Vocabulary Terms

larvae: a young form of an animal

locomotive: a powered rail vehicle used for pulling train cars

Mercury: a Roman messenger god known for his speed

meteor: a space rock that burns up in Earth's atmosphere

meteorite: a space rock that makes it all the way to the ground

microgravity: very low gravity; the reason astronauts float in space

mining: the process of obtaining metals and stones from the ground

monolith: a large stone all by itself

mound: the part of a termite colony that extends above the ground

mountain: a landform that rises higher than the surrounding area

mouth: the part of a river that empties into another body of water

orbit: the path of an object going around a star, planet, or other object in space

oxygen: a gas in the air that people need to live

particle: a really small piece of matter

planet: a spherical ball of rock and/or gas that orbits a star

pollute: to put harmful substances in the environment

polyp: a small underwater animal responsible for the creation of coral reefs

port: a harbor where ships load and unload before they sail to other countries to trade

predator: an animal that hunts and eats other animals

reticulated: something that looks like a net

satellite: an object in orbit

solar panel: a flat device that collects sunlight and turns it into energy

Space Race: the competition between the USA and the USSR to beat the other in space exploration

species: a group of similar animals with a common name

tarantula: a large, hairy spider

telescope: a tool that helps people see far away by collecting and focusing light

tentacles: long, slender, flexible limbs

termite: an insect that typically lives in colonies and feeds on wood

ton: 2,000 pounds

turbine: a machine with blades that spin when water flows over it, producing electricity

ungulate: a hoofed, cow-like animal

venom: a poisonous substance inside an animal

venomous: when an animal has a poisonous, or harmful, liquid inside of it

volume: the amount of space inside something

water pressure: the weight of water above and around something pushing on it

waterfall: where water in a stream falls over a drop in the terrain

Western Hemisphere: the Western half of the Earth, which includes North and South America

wingspan: the width of wings, from wingtip to wingtip

workers: pale termites that do most of the building and searching for food

Life Science

Dinosaurs

Students create full-size drawings of a Tyrannosaurus Rex and an Apatosaurus in order to see the size of these extinct giants.

Prepare

- *Allow time:* approximately 1 hour for this activity
- *Gather materials:* Plan 1, measuring tape or measuring wheel, sidewalk chalk

Focus

Dinosaurs have captured the imaginations of people for a very long time. They went extinct 65 million years ago. They were the biggest and baddest animals on land for nearly 160 million years! Many different types of dinosaurs existed. Two of the biggest were the Apatosaurus and the Tyrannosaurus Rex.

Present

❶ Consult Plan 1. On the playground (or appropriate indoor floor), draw a 43-foot line, and draw another, 13-foot line at a right angle to the end of the first line. Then complete the rectangle. Using the illustration as a guide, have students draw an outline of a Tyrannosaurus Rex inside the rectangle. Next, draw a 75-foot line and a 30-foot line at a right angle to the end of the first line. Complete the rectangle. Have students draw an outline of an Apatosaurus inside the second rectangle.

❷ The Apatosaurus was not always just called the Apatosaurus. A short time after it was first discovered, other scientists found another Apatosaurus skeleton and mistook it for a different species, which was named Brontosaurus. It was pointed out later that they were really the same. The name Brontosaurus has remained in use, however, in large part because people like it. Brontosaurus means "thunder lizard".

❸ The T-Rex is one of the largest land carnivores that ever lived. Scientists disagree, however, about how the T-Rex got meat to eat. Some scientists think T-Rex was a predator and caught other animals. Other scientists think T-Rex was a scavenger and mainly ate animals that were already dead.

——————— Vocabulary ———————

dinosaur: any member of a group of lizard-like animals varying greatly in size that roamed the Earth for 160 million years

Conclude

The name Tyrannosaurus Rex is a very impressive name. Tyrannosaurus means "tyrant lizard," and Rex means "king." Put those two words together and you get "tyrant lizard king." Discuss with students why scientists give dinosaurs names like "tyrant lizard king" and "thunder lizard." Ask students what they would name a dinosaur if they discovered a new one.

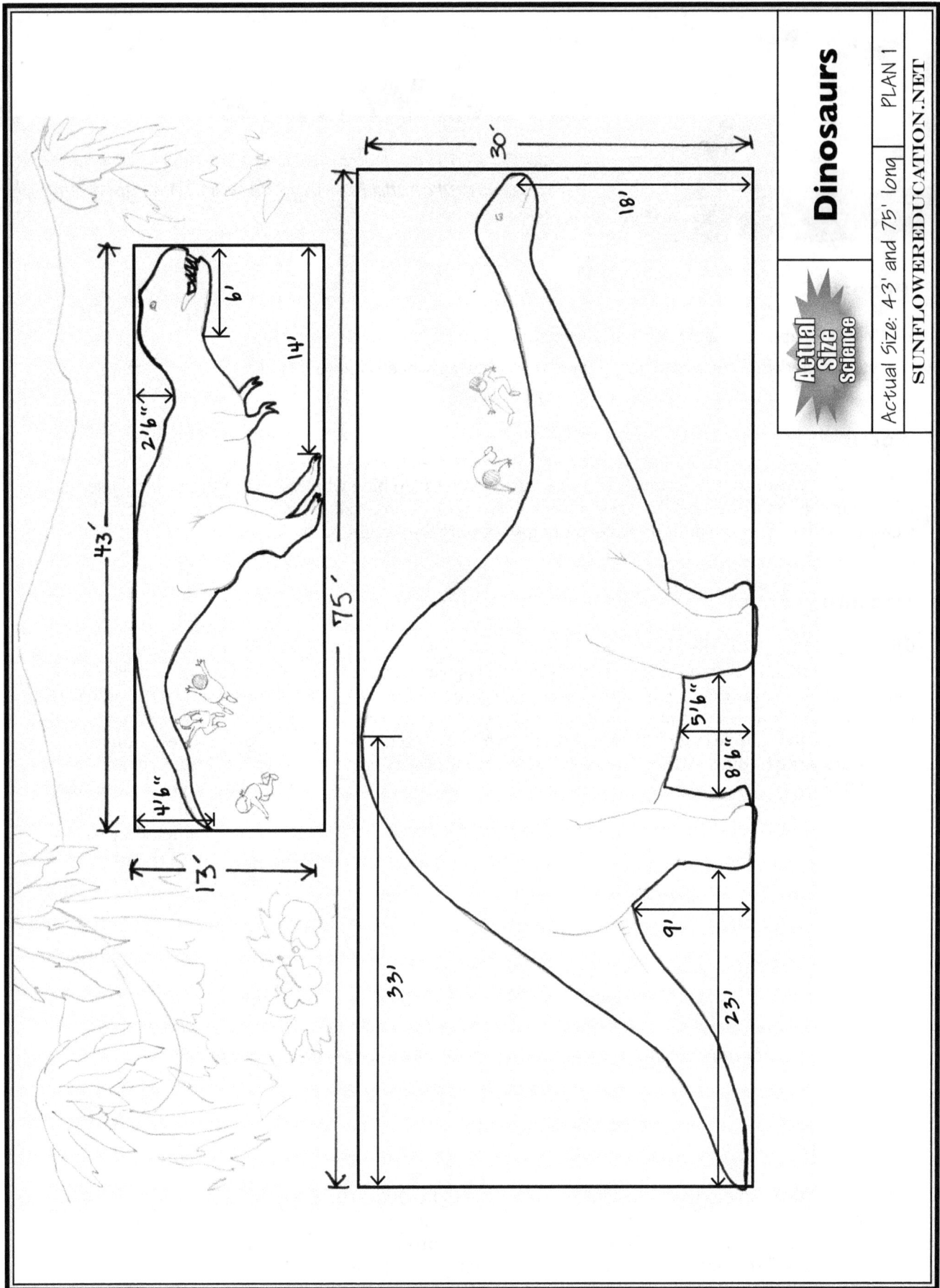

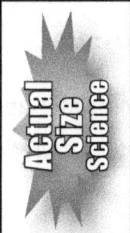

Dinosaurs

Actual Size: 43' and 75' long | PLAN 1

Actual Size Science

SUNFLOWEREDUCATION.NET

30'

18'

43'

14'

6'

2'6"

4'6"

13'

75'

33'

23'

9'

5'6"

8'6"

Blue Whale

Students create a full-scale drawing of a blue whale in order to comprehend how big the world's largest animal can be.

Prepare

- *Allow time:* approximately 30 minutes for this activity
- *Gather materials:* Plan 2, measuring tape or measuring wheel, sidewalk chalk

Focus

What is the world's largest animal? The blue whale! Where do blue whales live? In the ocean. Discuss with your class why the world's largest animal lives in the ocean. Ask "where do you feel lighter, in the water or on land?" The water in the ocean helps support the weight of the blue whale.

Present

❶ Consult Plan 2. On the playground (or appropriate indoor floor), draw a 108-foot line. Using this line as the center of the blue whale, guide students as they draw the outline of the blue whale.

❷ This is an outline of the largest blue whale ever recorded by people. Can you guess how heavy it was? A whopping 190 tons! A blue whale is so big that its heart is the same size as some small cars!

❸ What does an animal this big eat? Sharks? Sea turtles? Giant fish? Surprisingly, the blue whale, the largest animal on Earth, eats one of the smallest animals on our planet, *krill*. Krill are tiny shrimp-like animals. Blue whales don't have teeth; instead they have *baleen*, which they use to strain krill out of the water. A blue whale can eat as many as 40 million krill in a day!

—————————— Vocabulary ——————————

krill: a small shrimp-like animal that lives in the ocean
baleen: rows of hard plates that hang down from the upper jaw of some whales
endangered: a species threatened to go extinct, or disappear completely

Conclude

Talk with students about what it means for an animal to be *endangered*. Before we learned how to use oil from the ground, people hunted down whales to use the oil from their bodies. So many whales were killed that they were in danger of disappearing forever. Fortunately, today, there are people who look out for blue whales and other types of whales and are trying to help their numbers grow again.

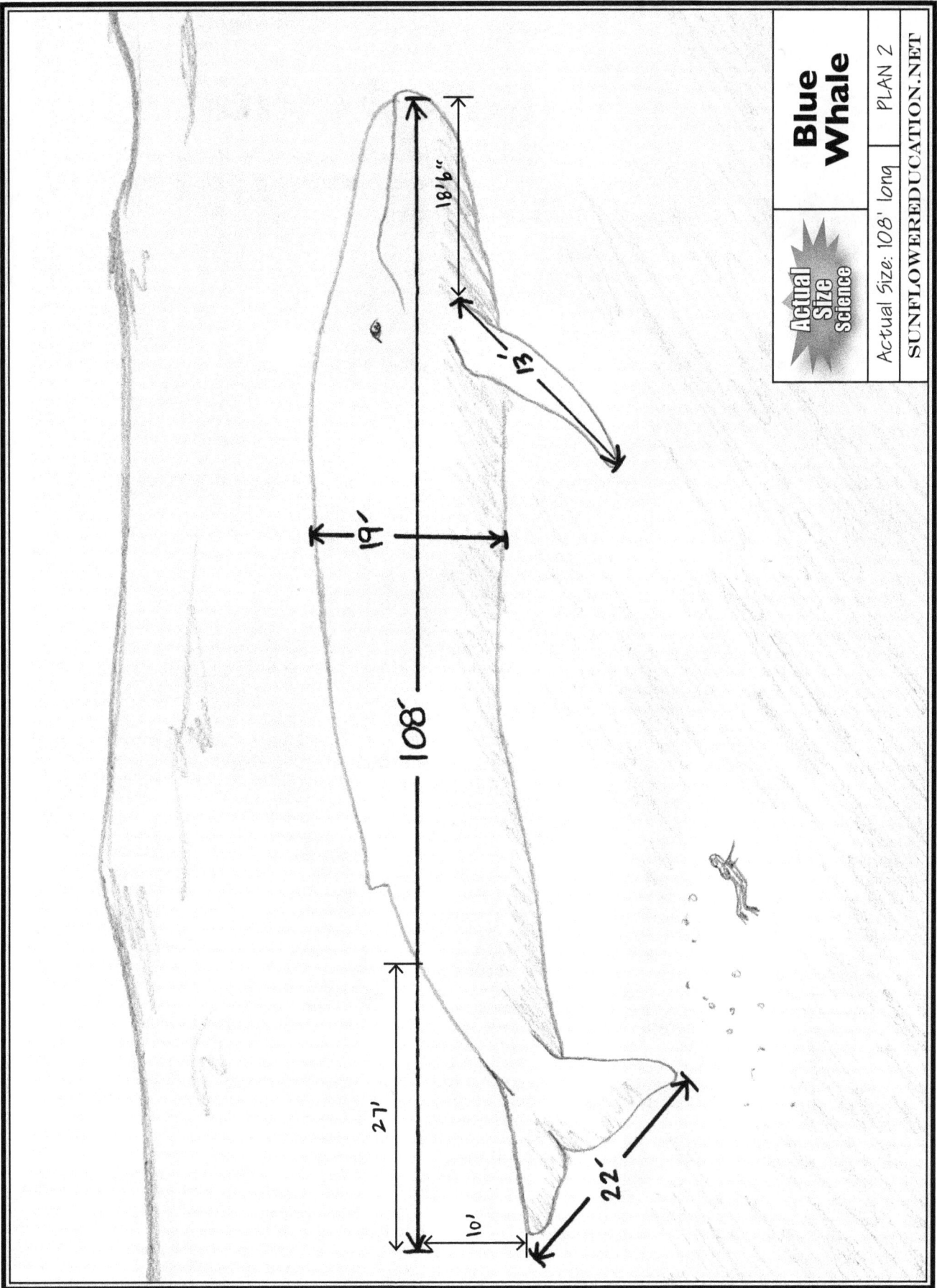

Blue Whale

PLAN 2

SUNFLOWEREDUCATION.NET

Actual Size Science

Actual Size: 108' long

18'6"

13'

19'

108'

27'

22'

10'

Activity 3
Giant Squid

Students create a life-sized outline of a giant squid in order to see the size of the animal that inspired the story of the Kraken.

Prepare

- *Allow time:* approximately 30 minutes for this activity
- *Gather materials:* Plan 3, measuring tape or measuring wheel, sidewalk chalk

Focus

Sailors have told stories about giant creatures living in the ocean for a very long time. One of these creatures was called the Kraken. Many people now think that the stories about this tentacled monster were created by those who had actually seen a giant squid.

Present

❶ Consult Plan 3. On the playground (or appropriate indoor floor), draw a 43-foot line. Using the illustration as a guide, have students draw an outline of a giant squid around the line.

❷ For a very long time, scientists thought that the giant squid was a myth made up by sailors. The first recorded proof of the giant squid in recent history occurred in 1861 when a French ship brought back a tentacle of a giant squid they encountered at sea. Since that time, scientists have found whole giant squid and even taken live videos of them.

❸ Giant squid eat fish and other sea animals. They use their two long *tentacles* to capture their prey. Suckers on their tentacles provide grip. They then pull what they caught to their mouth, which is actually a large beak, like a bird has.

―――――――――― Vocabulary ――――――――――

tentacles: a long, slender, flexible limbs
water pressure: the weight of water above and around something pushing on it

Conclude

Giant squid live in some of the deepest parts of the ocean. They live so deep that the *water pressure* makes it very hard for people to go down that far. Because of this, it is very difficult for scientists to study the giant squid. Like other squid, giant squid use their tentacles to catch food such as fish and smaller squid. The only thing known to eat giant squid is the sperm whale.

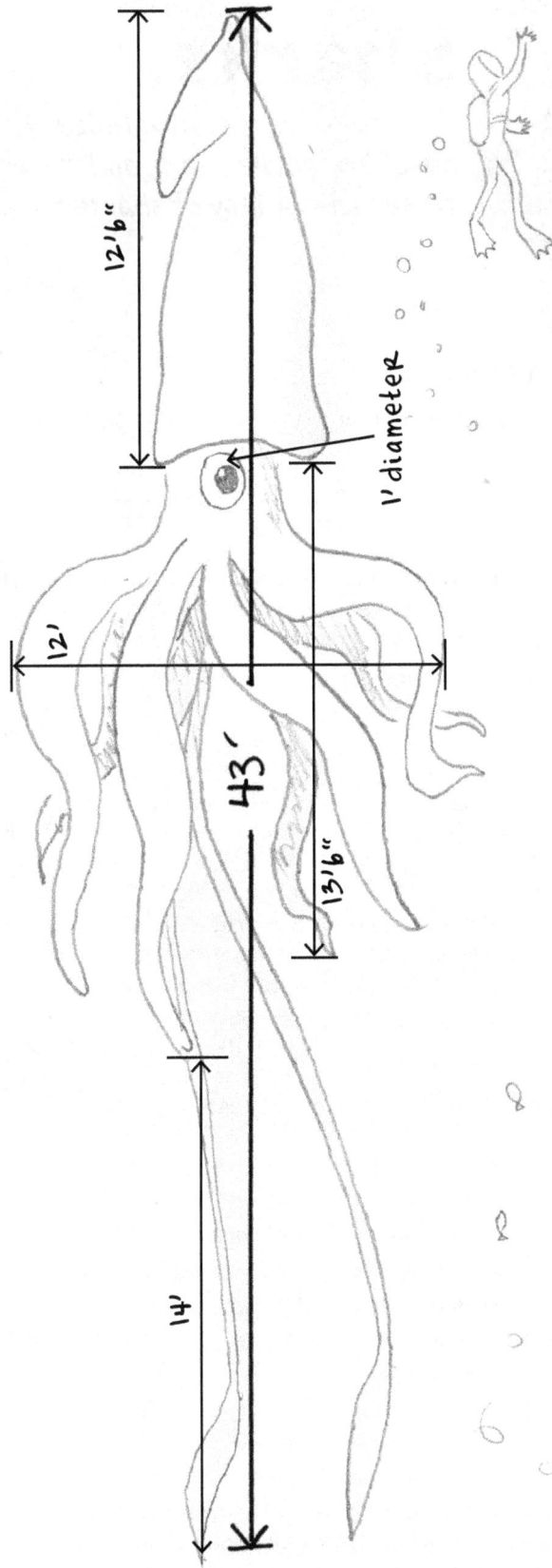

Giant Squid

PLAN 3

Actual Size Science

Actual Size: 43' long

SUNFLOWEREDUCATION.NET

12' 6"

1' diameter

12'

43'

13' 6"

14'

Activity 4
Sharks

Students create actual-size drawings of the pale catshark, whale shark, and the great white shark in order to see the variety of sharks that inhabit our oceans.

Prepare

- *Allow time:* approximately 1½ hours for this activity
- *Gather materials:* Plan 4, ruler, measuring tape or measuring wheel, sidewalk chalk

Focus

What is one of the oldest types of animals on Earth? Sharks! The oldest sharks we know about were around before the dinosaurs—420 million years ago! Since that time, many different species of sharks have evolved throughout all of the world's oceans.

Present

❶ Consult Plan 4. On the playground (or appropriate indoor floor), draw three parallel lines with at least 5 feet between each line. The pale catshark line should be 8.25 inches long, the great white shark line should be 20 feet long, and the whale shark line should be 41 feet and 6 inches long. Using the illustration as a guide, have students draw an outline of each shark around its respective line.

❷ Two of these sharks eat fish of about the same size. Can you guess which two? If you guessed the whale shark and the pale catshark, you were right! The pale catshark, being very little, eats extremely little things. The whale shark, despite being huge, only eats very little fish and krill. The great white shark, on the other hand, mainly eats seals and large fish.

❸ Many people are scared of sharks, but we don't need to be. In the whole world, there are around only 100 reported shark attacks in a year, and 9 out of 10 of those people survive. It is much more likely for someone to get struck by lightening than to die from a shark attack. Sharks have more reason to fear people than we have to fear them. Every year between 100 and 200 million sharks are killed by people.

———————————— Vocabulary ————————————

extinct: no longer exists or lives anywhere
adapted: well-suited to the world around you
predator: an animal that hunts and eats other animals

Conclude

Sharks are some of the oldest animals on the planet. Discuss with students why sharks have lasted as long as they have while other species have gone *extinct*. Sharks are very well *adapted* for their lives as *predators*. Their shape lets them move very quickly through the water, and their excellent senses and sharp teeth make them very good predators.

2"

8.25"

7'

2'

5'6"

5'3"

4'

20'

18'3"

4'

14'

41'6"

7'

8'3"

8'

4'

7'3"

Actual Size Science

Sharks

Actual Size: 8.25", 20', 41' 6" long

PLAN 4

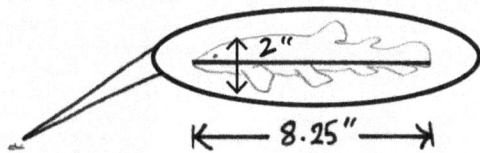

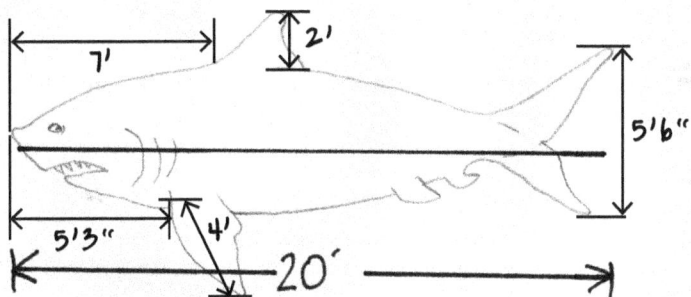

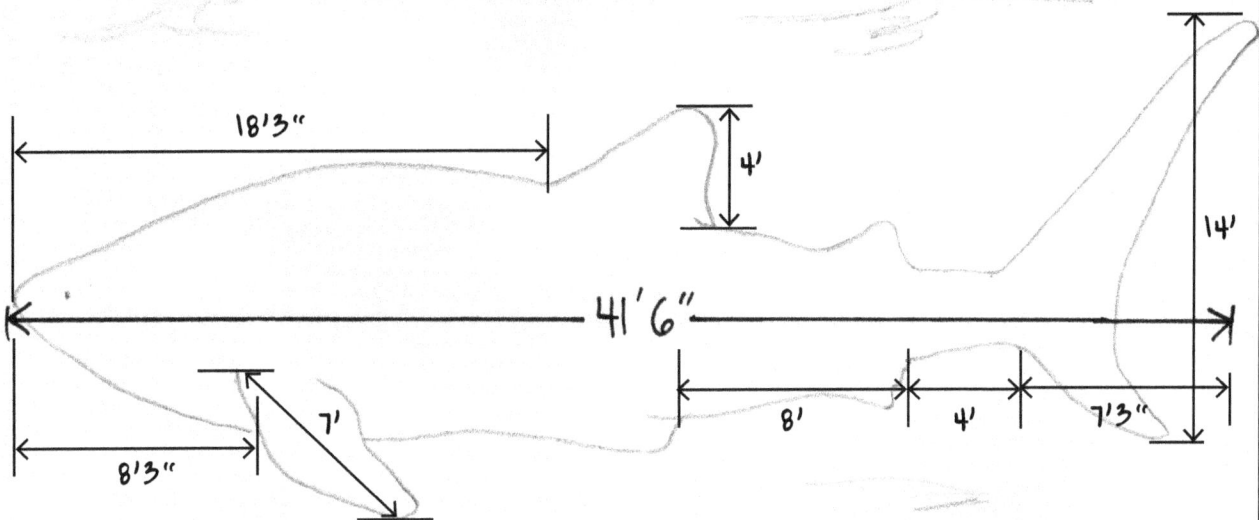

Activity 5
Polar Bear

Students create a full-scale drawing of a polar bear in order to appreciate the size of the world's largest land carnivore.

Prepare

- *Allow time:* approximately 45 minutes for this activity
- *Gather materials:* Plan 5, measuring stick or measuring wheel, sidewalk chalk

Focus

What is the weather like at the top of the world? Extremely cold! This may make it surprising that the biggest *carnivore* on land lives in the *Arctic*. Polar bears live and thrive in this extreme part of the Earth.

Present

❶ Consult Plan 5. On the playground (or appropriate indoor floor), draw a 9-foot, 10 inch line, and draw another line 5 feet long at a right angle to the end of the first line. Then complete the rectangle. Using the illustration as a guide, have students draw an outline of a polar bear within the rectangle.

❷ Polar bears have several important adaptations that help them live in the Arctic. They have two layers of fur that help trap heat inside their bodies and keep out water when they swim. Underneath their fur, polar bears have thick layers of blubber that also help keep heat from escaping their bodies.

❸ Unlike a lot of other carnivores around the world, polar bears do some of their best hunting during the winter. Can you guess why? Because polar bears like to hunt seals in the ocean. During the winter, there is a lot of ice on the surface of the Arctic Ocean that polar bears can walk on to better hunt seals.

———————————— Vocabulary ————————————

carnivore: an animal that eats other animals
Arctic: the top of the Earth around the North Pole
global warming: the gradual warming of the Earth's atmosphere caused by people

Conclude

Polar bears were once over hunted. They became scarce, but laws protecting polar bears have helped them come back. Recently, scientists have found a new threat to the survival of polar bears. Many scientists fear that *global warming* is reducing the amount of ice in the Arctic. Polar bears depend on the sea ice to stand on. Why do you think people want to protect animals like polar bears?

© 2013 Sunflower Education

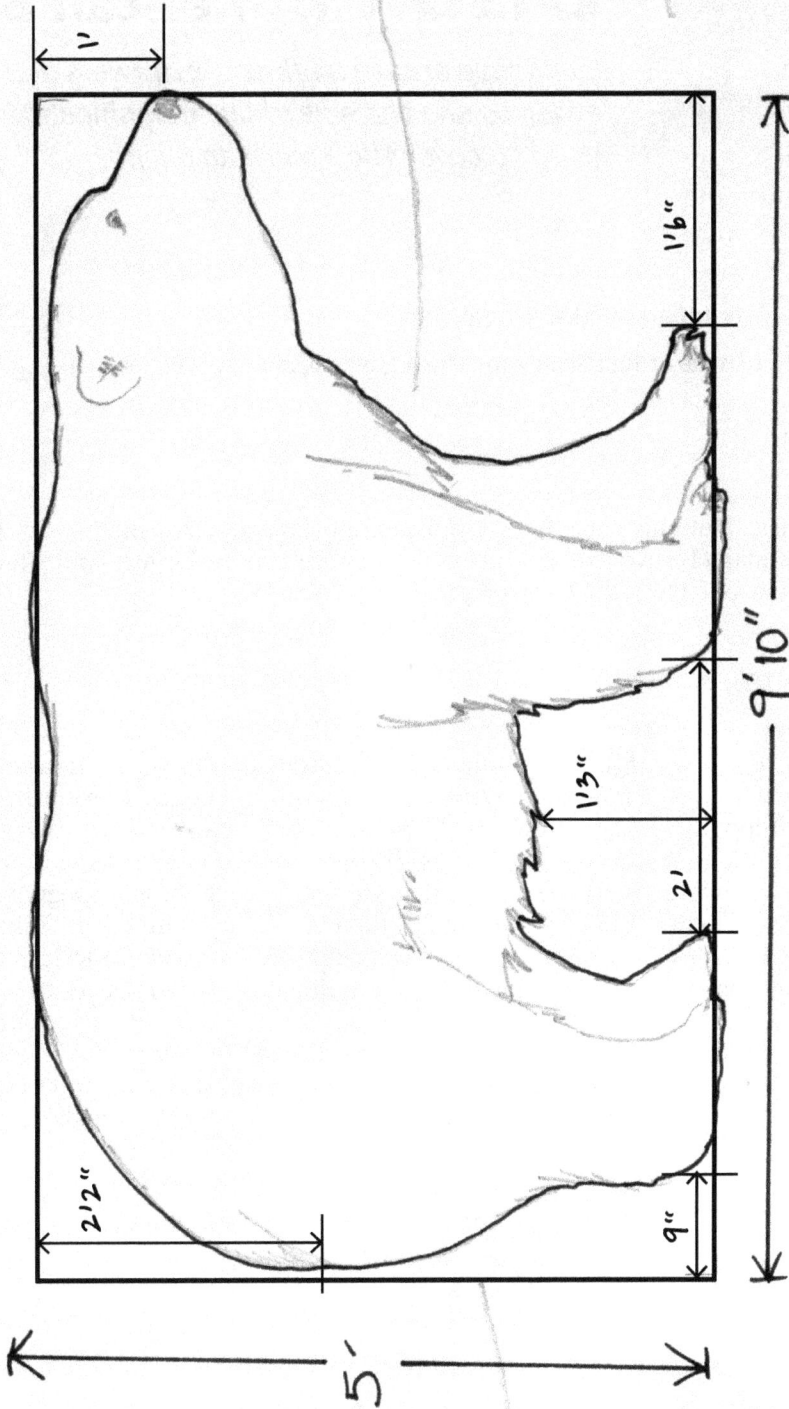

Polar Bear

Actual Size Science

Actual Size: 9'10" x 5'

PLAN 5

SUNFLOWEREDUCATION.NET

1'

1'6"

9'10"

1'3"

2'

2'2"

9"

5'

Bison (American Buffalo)

Students create a full-scale drawing of a bison in order to see the size of the magnificent animal that used to cover the American plains.

Prepare

- *Allow time:* approximately 1 hour for this activity
- *Gather materials:* Plan 6, measuring stick or measuring wheel, sidewalk chalk, scale figures

Focus

Bison are a pretty big deal. Not only have they played an important role in history—they were once the main source of food for many Native American tribes—they are also the largest land animal in America. A bison can weigh anywhere from 1,200 to 1,800 pounds!

Present

❶ Consult Plan 6. On the playground (or appropriate indoor floor), draw a 10-foot line, and draw another line 6 feet and 6 inches long at a right angle to the end of the first line. Then complete the rectangle. Using the illustration as a guide, have students draw an outline of a bison within the rectangle.

❷ It is estimated that before 1600 there were 30-70 million bison in North America. Over the next 300 years, European settlers reduced that number to fewer than 1,000. Today, bison *herds* are protected in Yellowstone and other national parks. Many people also raise bison on private ranches. Today there are about 450,000 bison in North America.

❸ Bison herds could be huge—one herd could cover 400 square miles and include tens of millions of animals. One herd was allegedly the size of Connecticut. Take a copy of the Native American and smaller bison figures to a football field. In scale, large herds were often the size of the football field— and sometimes the size of *four* football fields!

——————————— Vocabulary ———————————
herd: a group of animals living together
ungulate: a hoofed, cow-like animal

Conclude

Bison are more commonly called Buffalo or American Buffalo. Discuss with students why scientists call them bison. There are other *ungulates* called buffalo in Asia and Africa. American Bison are less like those buffalo and more like an animal in Europe called the European Bison.

Bison

PLAN 6

Actual Size: 10' x 6' 6"

SUNFLOWEREDUCATION.NET

Actual Size Science

I" to-scale figure

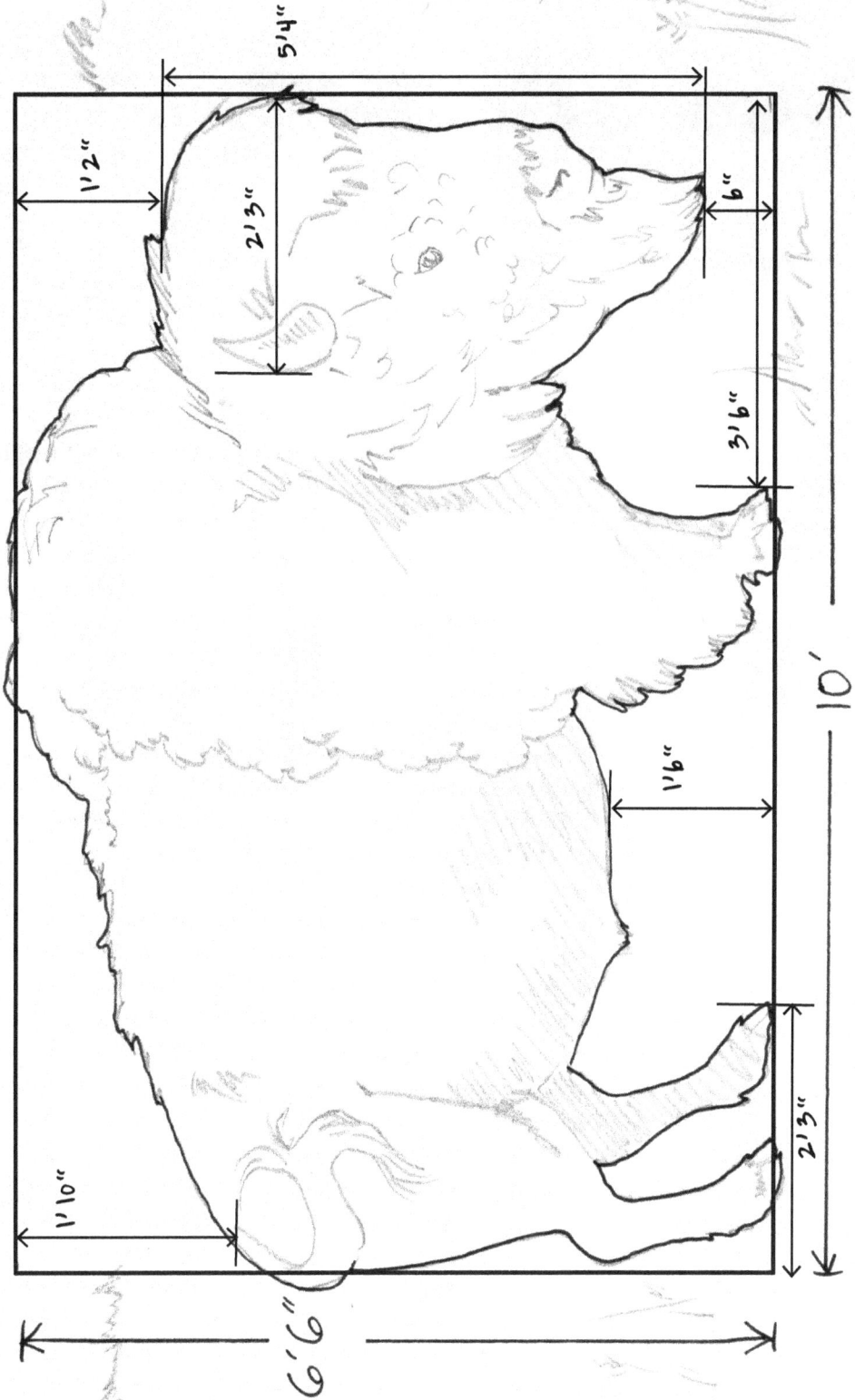

5'4"

1'2"

2'3"

6"

3'6"

1'9"

10'

2'3"

1'10"

6'6"

Activity 7
Elephant

Students create a full-size drawing of an elephant in order to appreciate the size of the world's biggest land animal.

Prepare

- *Allow time:* approximately 1 hour for this activity
- *Gather materials:* Plan 7, measuring stick or measuring wheel, sidewalk chalk

Focus

What is the biggest animal on land today? If you said elephant, you're exactly right! There are bigger animals in the ocean, but on land nothing is bigger than the African elephant.

Present

❶ Consult Plan 7. On the playground (or appropriate indoor floor), draw a 24-foot line. Draw another line that is 10 feet and 10 inches long at a right angle to the end of the first line. Then complete the rectangle. Using the illustration as a guide, have students draw an outline of an elephant within the rectangle.

❷ Elephants have very special noses, called trunks. Elephants use them for all kinds of things: as a nose, hand, extra leg, snorkel when swimming, and a straw when drinking. Discuss with students what it would be like to have a trunk. Would life be easier or harder?

❸ Have students spend time in the outline of the elephant. Talk with them about how heavy an elephant is: up to 26,000 pounds (13 tons)! They must support all of that weight on their feet. This is one of the reasons why they have such huge tree-trunk legs. Their feet also expand when they step to spread their weight out.

—————————— Vocabulary ——————————
species: a group of similar animals with a common name

Conclude

Talk with students about the different *species* of elephants. The world's largest land animal is the African elephant. There are also Asian elephants (a.k.a. Indian elephants) which are slightly smaller than African elephants. Both species of elephants are named after the area of the world where they live. An easy way to tell them apart is by looking at their ears. African elephants have big ears that are in the shape of Africa! Asian elephants have smaller ears in the shape of India.

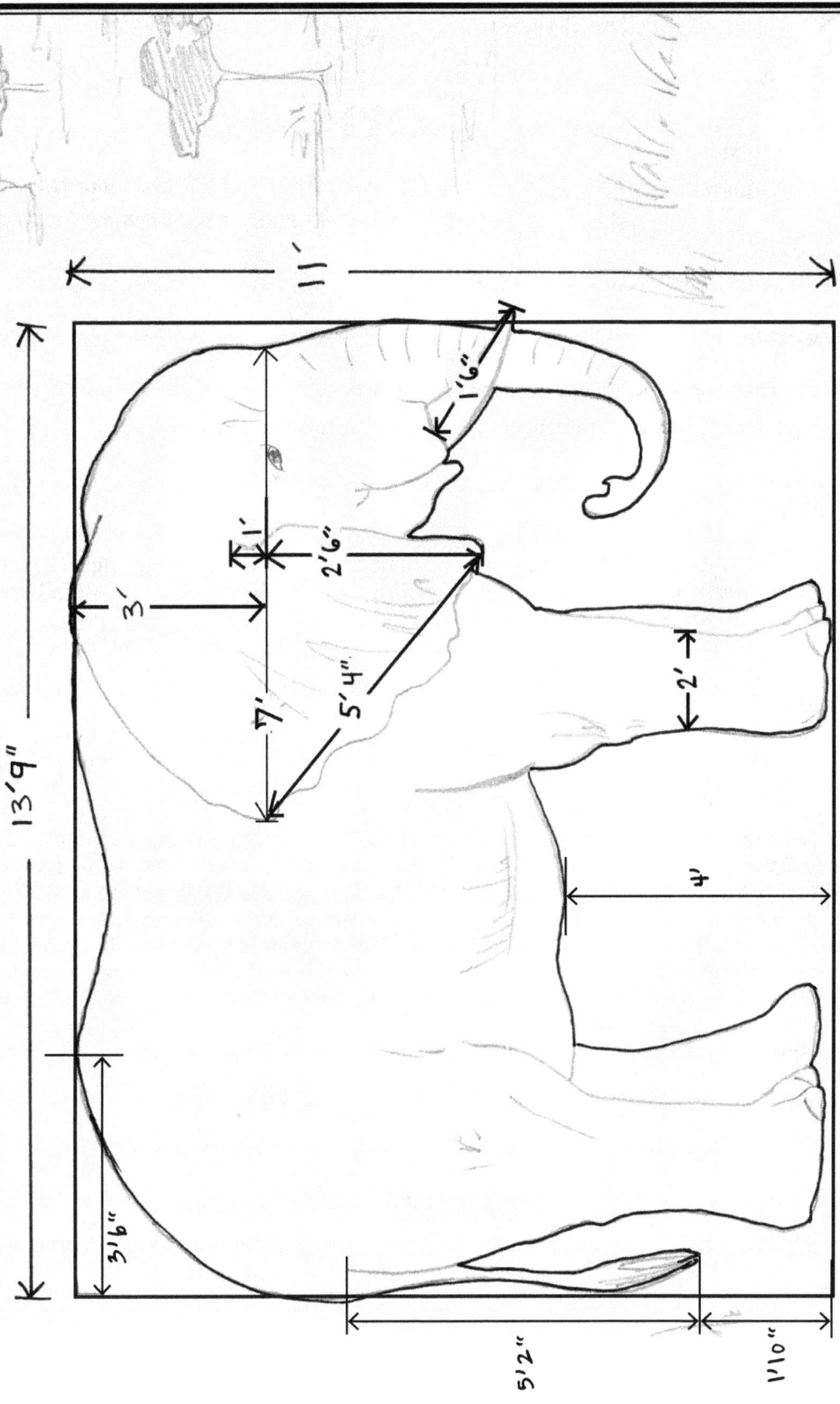

Elephant

PLAN 7

Actual Size: 13' 9" x 11"

SUNFLOWEREDUCATION.NET

13'9"

11'

3'

1'

2'6"

7'

5'4"

1'6"

2'

4'

3'6"

5'2"

1'10"

Condor

Students create an outline of a condor in order to appreciate the size of this majestic bird.

Prepare

- *Allow time:* approximately 30 minutes for this activity
- *Gather materials:* Plan 8, measuring stick or measuring wheel, sidewalk chalk

Focus

Who hasn't looked up at the sky and wanted to be a bird? Now imagine seeing an American condor soaring above. Its *wingspan* is nearly ten feet! This bird, which lives in the Western United States and Mexico, is the largest flying land bird in North America.

Present

❶ Consult Plan 8. On the playground (or appropriate indoor floor), draw a line that is 9 feet 6 inches long. Through the middle of this line, draw a line that is 4 feet 2 inches long and perpendicular to the first line. These are the dimensions of an American condor. Using the illustration as a guide, have students draw an outline of this large bird.

❷ The American condor has a cousin, the Andean condor. The Andean condor lives in Peru and is a little bit shorter than the American condor, but its wingspan is even longer. Together, these two birds are the biggest flying land birds in the *Western Hemisphere*. Both birds fly vast distances—as much as 150 miles a day, in search of food. They are such good gliders that they flap their wings only an average of one time per hour!

❸ Condors eat *carrion*, or animals which are already dead. They don't find food everyday, but when they do, they really eat! Sometimes, a condor will not be able to lift itself off the ground to fly after it eats, because it is so full. The life span of many animals is much shorter than the average human. Many condors, though, may live up to 50 years. The oldest condor ever lived to be 100!

—————————— *Vocabulary* ——————————
wingspan: the width of wings, from wingtip to wingtip
Western Hemisphere: the Western half of the Earth, which includes North and South America
carrion: animals that are already dead

Conclude

Have students work as partners to compare their "wingspan" to that of a condor. Have students spread their arms as far apart as possible, and their partner should measure the distance between the fingertips of each hand. A student's "wingspan" will probably be a lot less than the condor's!

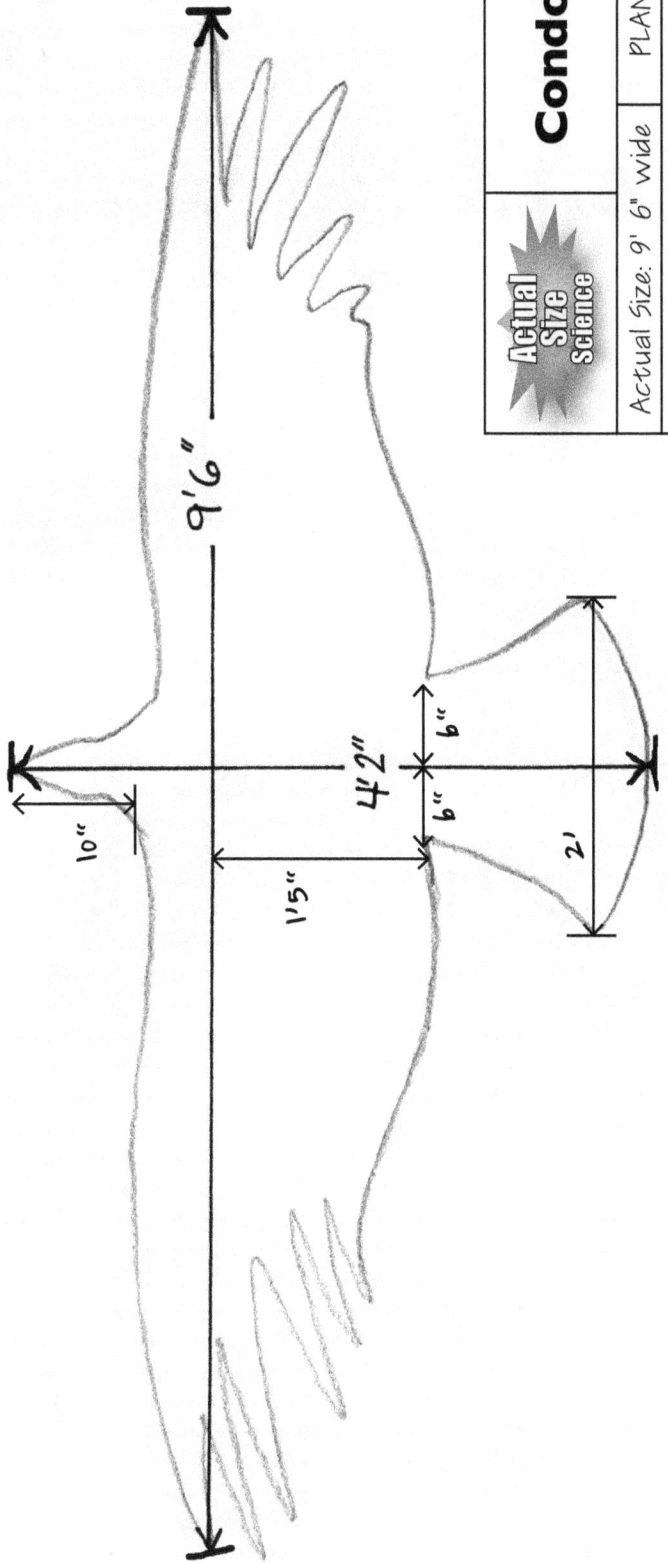

Condor

Actual Size Science

Actual Size: 9' 6" wide

PLAN B

SUNFLOWEREDUCATION.NET

9'6"

42"

1'5"

10"

6"

6"

2'

Activity 9
Tallest Tree

Students create an outline of the world's tallest tree, the National Geographic Society Redwood Tree, in order to appreciate the height of the tallest tree in the world.

Prepare

- *Allow time:* approximately 30 minutes for this activity
- *Gather materials:* Plan 9, measuring tape or measuring wheel, sidewalk chalk

Focus

Trees are some of the most common plants in the world. You might see many of them everyday. How tall can trees get? Currently, the tallest kind of tree is the redwood tree. Redwoods grow along the West Coast of the United States. The tallest living redwood is the National Geographic Society Redwood Tree. This particular redwood is 365 feet and 6 inches tall. That's taller than the Statue of Liberty!

Present

❶ Consult Plan 9. On the playground, draw a line 365 feet and 6 inches long. Draw another line 26 feet long at a right angle to the end of the first line. Then complete the rectangle. Using the illustration as a guide, have students draw an outline of the branches of the redwood around the rectangle.

❷ To create a more manageable, quarter-scale diagram, draw a rectangle 91 feet 3 inches by 6 feet 6 inches.

❸ The National Geographic Society Redwood Tree is the tallest tree in the world today. Many scientists, though, think that a short while ago there were several taller trees. For example, in Australia there was a Eucalyptus tree that people believed to be more than 400 feet tall!

——————— *Vocabulary* ———————
volume: the amount of space inside something

Conclude

The National Geographic Society Redwood Tree is the world's tallest tree, but can you guess what kind of tree is the world's largest by *volume?* The sequoia is a very close relative of the redwood tree. Sequoias do not grow as tall as redwoods, but Sequoias grow much wider. The biggest tree by volume is a sequoia called the General Sherman Tree in Sequoia National Park, California. The diameter of this tree's trunk is 37.3 feet!

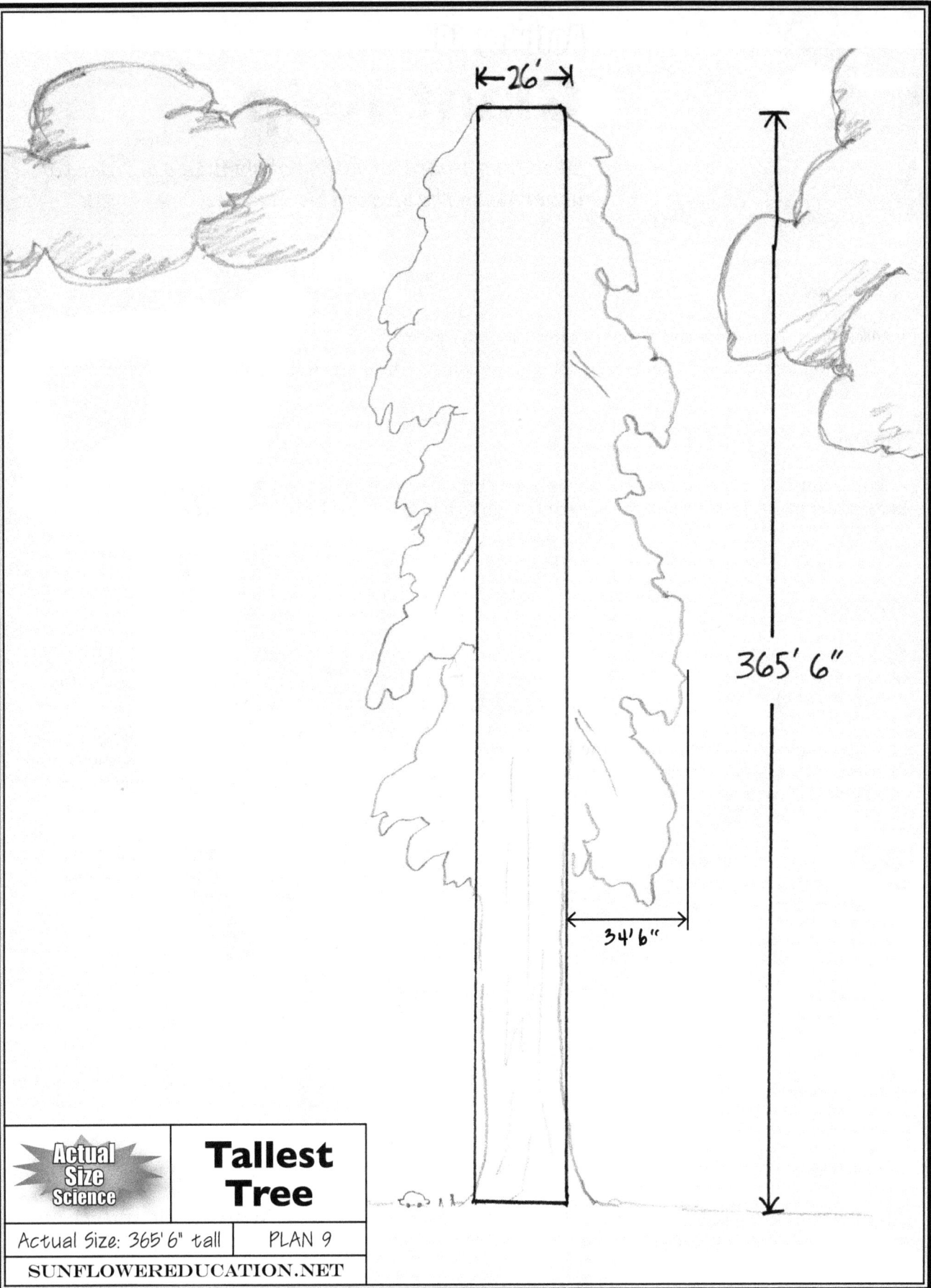

← 26' →

365' 6"

34' 6"

Actual Size Science

Tallest Tree

Actual Size: 365' 6" tall   PLAN 9

SUNFLOWEREDUCATION.NET

Giant Kelp

Students create an outline of giant kelp in order to understand the size of this seaweed.

Prepare

- *Allow time:* approximately 30 minutes for this activity
- *Gather materials:* Plan 10, measuring tape or measuring wheel, sidewalk chalk

Focus

Ask students how many inches they have grown in the past year. Then explain to them that giant kelp, a kind of plant that grows in the ocean, can grow up to two feet a day! Imagine if a person could grow that quickly!

Present

❶ Consult Plan 10. On the playground (or appropriate indoor floor), draw a 108-foot line. Draw a second, 42-foot line at a right angle at one end of the first line. Using the illustration as a guide, have students draw a picture of a giant kelp.

❷ When several kelp grow near each other, they form a kelp forest. These underwater forests are home to many kinds of sea creatures, because the kelp provides both food and shelter to these creatures. The top part of the kelp, the *canopy,* is home to many very small organisms and *larvae.* The leaves on the kelp help keep these animals from floating away. Different kinds of fish hang out beneath the canopy, snacking on the small sea creatures they like to eat.

Small, *invertebrate* animals, like sea sponges, live in the bottom section of the plant.

❸ Did you know that people eat seaweed, too? A substance found in kelp is used to make gooey things like ice cream and salad dressing. Other kinds of seaweed can be eaten directly and are very good for you—as well as tasty.

─────────── Vocabulary ───────────

canopy: the top part of the kelp
larvae: a young form of an animal
invertebrate: an animal without a backbone

Conclude

Ask students how tall they would be if they grew two feet a day for a week. Measure their current heights, and then add the amount they would grow if they grew as fast as giant kelp. They would probably be pretty tall! Would it be fun to be that tall?

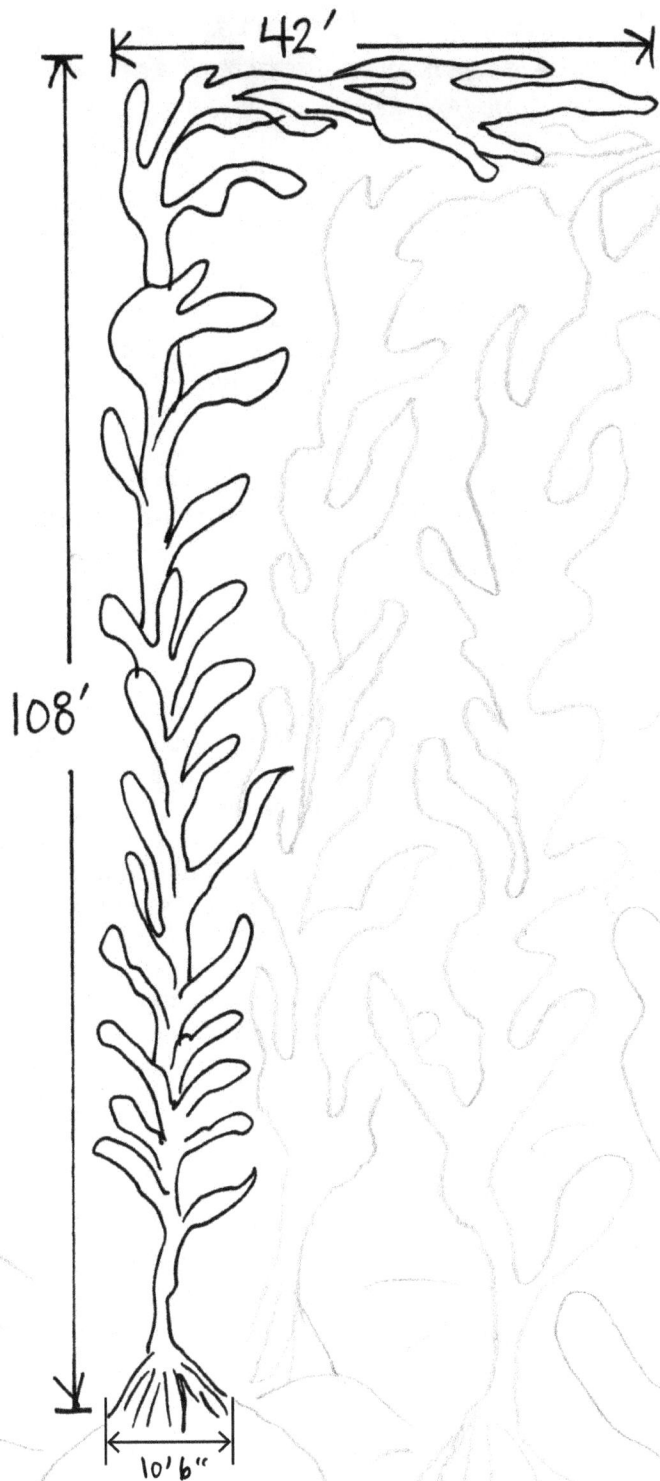

42'

108'

10' 6"

Actual Size Science

Giant Kelp

Actual Size: 108' tall   PLAN 10

SUNFLOWEREDUCATION.NET

Termite Mound

Students create an outline of a termite mound in order to see the impressive size of a structure created entirely by insects.

Prepare

- *Allow time:* approximately 30 minutes for this activity
- *Gather materials:* Plan 11, measuring tape or measuring wheel, sidewalk chalk

Focus

Explain to students that *termites* are insects that look sort of like ants. They eat plants and wood. There are many different types of termites. Some types live in wood. Other types live in soil. The soil-dwelling termites of Africa and Australia build mounds out of soil and chewed woods. Most are six to ten feet tall, but the tallest ones are 30 feet high; as tall as a three-story building!

Present

❶ Consult Plan 11. On the playground (or appropriate indoor floor), sketch a circle, or oval 8 feet in diameter. This represents the base of the mound. From its center, draw a 30 foot line. Use the line as a guide to sketch the mound.

❷ Millions of termites can live in a single mound. Have students imagine what it would be like to live in a termite mound. If a *worker* termite is .25" long, how big would a termite mound be if it were made by termites the size of people? More than one mile and a half tall!

❸ Gather students "inside" the termite mound. Explain that termite mounds are complex structures with many chambers and ventilation shafts. They are home to millions of termites of the colony. The colony includes a king and a queen, workers who build the mound and clean it (and gather food and water), and soldiers who guard the mound from ants.

—————————————— Vocabulary ——————————————

termite: an insect that typically lives in colonies and feeds on wood
mound: the part of a termite colony that extends above the ground
workers: pale termites that do most of the building and searching for food

Conclude

Talk with students about why we don't have any buildings over a mile in diameter. We don't know how to build a stable structure that big, nor do we have a way to effectively keep the air moving through a building that huge. We have air conditioning and electricity, but there are some things that termites are better at than we are.

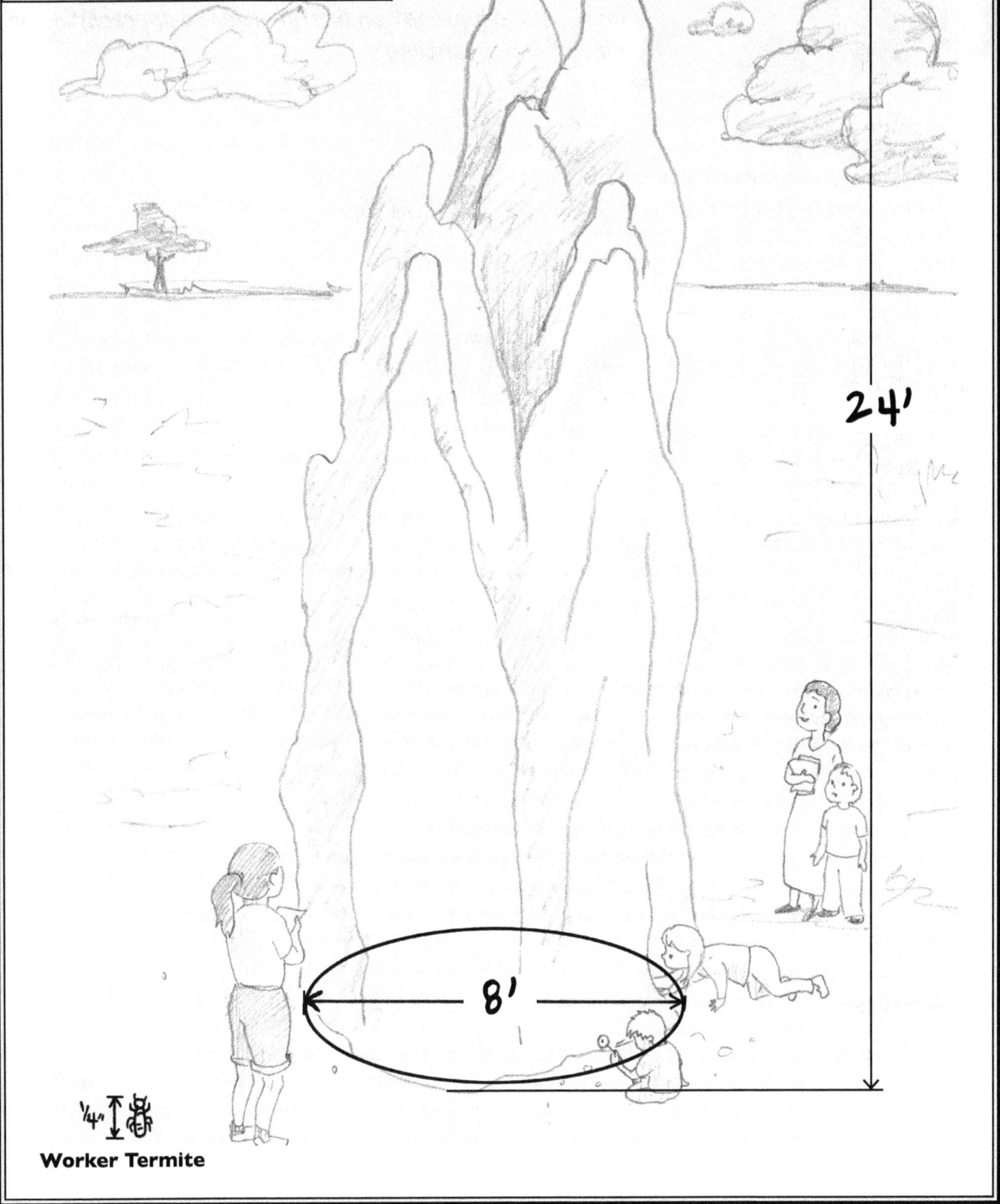

24'

8'

¼" **Worker Termite**

Biggest Snakes

Students create life-sized drawings of the world's longest and heaviest snakes in order to appreciate the size of these reptiles.

Prepare

- *Allow time:* approximately 1 hour for this activity
- *Gather materials:* Plan 12, measuring tape or measuring wheel, sidewalk chalk

Focus

What is the world's biggest snake? There are actually two of them. The world's longest snake, the *reticulated* python, can be up to 33 feet long! This kind of snake is pretty skinny, though, so the green anaconda is considered to be the world's heaviest snake.

Present

❶ Consult Plan 12. On the playground (or appropriate indoor floor), draw a 33-foot line. Using the illustration as a guide, have students draw an outline of a snake. This is the reticulated python. At a little distance from the first picture, draw a 28-foot line. Using the illustration as a guide, draw an outline of a snake that is 3 feet 8 inches wide at its widest point. This is the green anaconda.

❷ These snakes have a few things in common. Not only are they both really big, they also are both good swimmers. The reticulated python even swims in the ocean and can *colonize* nearby islands. Neither of them are *venomous*. Instead, they get their food by squeezing their prey really, really tightly.

❸ These snakes might be pretty scary, but we don't really need to worry about them. They both live far away—the reticulated python in Asia and the green anaconda in South America.

_____ Vocabulary _____

reticulated: something that looks like a net
colonize: to settle in a new place
venomous: when an animal has a poisonous, or harmful, liquid inside of it

Conclude

The reticulated python is named that because the patterns on its skin look like a net. Have students come up with creative designs for the "skins" of their snakes. Let each student draw their pattern on a small patch of the snake. Since these snakes are so big, there should be plenty of room!

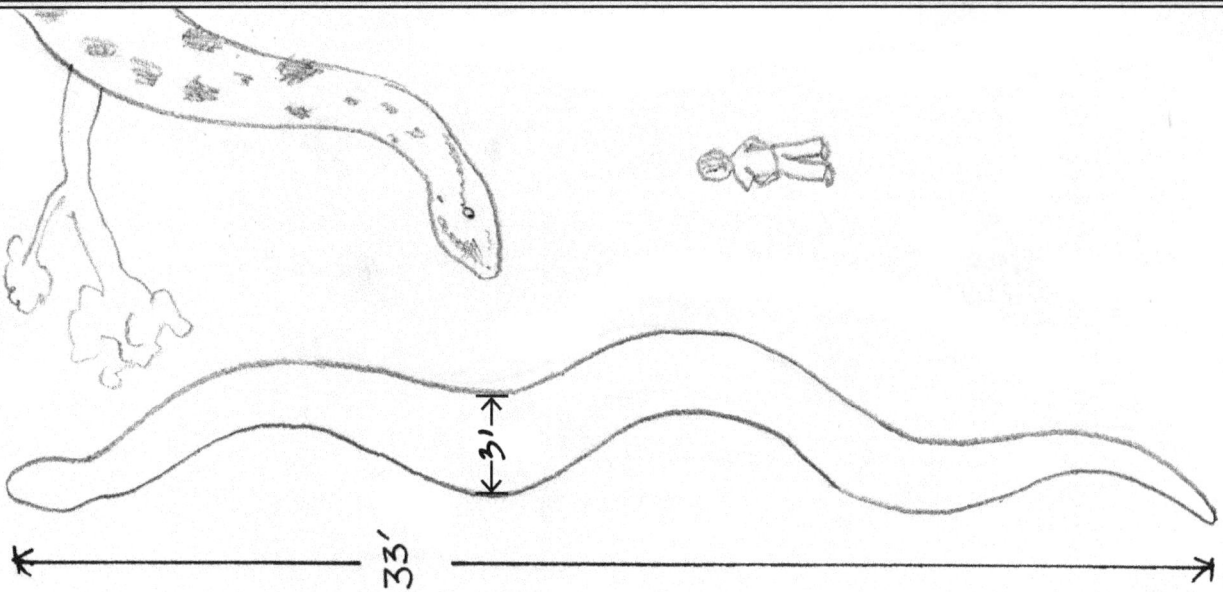

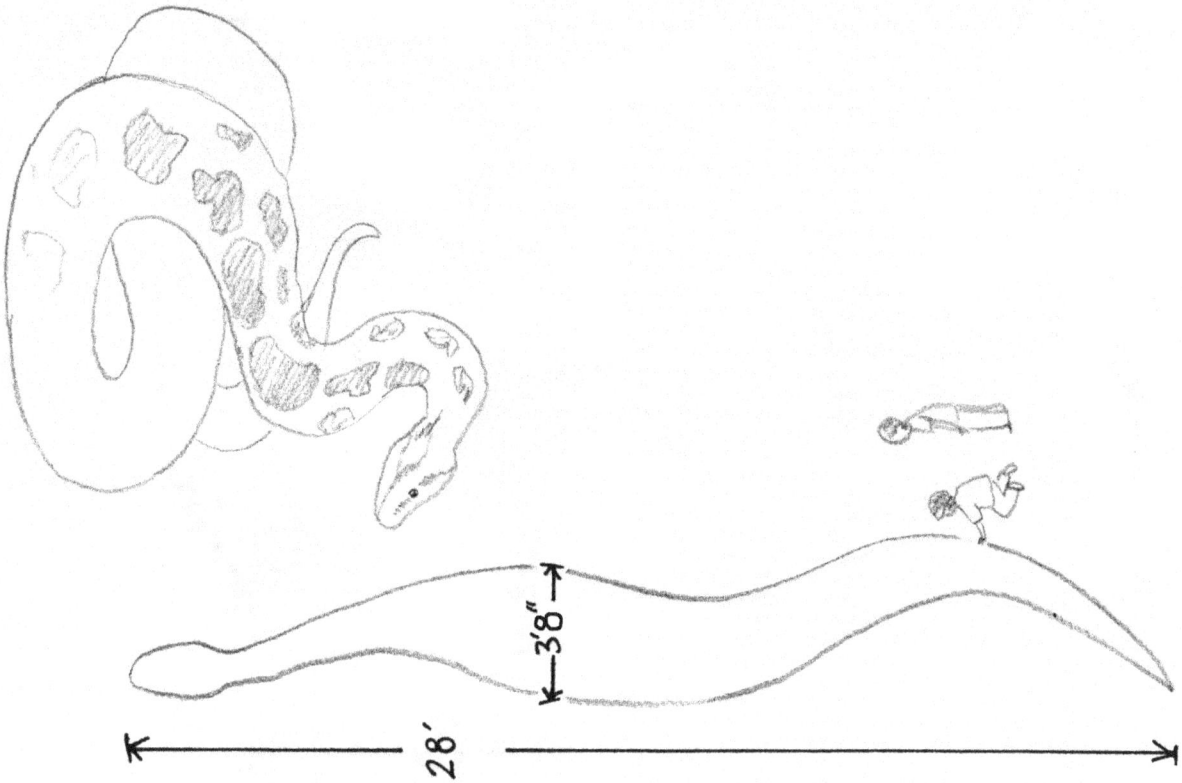

3'

33'

3'8"

28'

Actual Size Science

Biggest Snakes

Actual Size: 28' and 33' long | PLAN 12

SUNFLOWEREDUCATION.NET

|

Activity 13
Biggest Spider

Students create a life-sized outline of the world's biggest spider in order to appreciate its size.

Prepare

- *Allow time:* approximately 45 minutes for this activity
- *Gather materials:* Plan 13, measuring stick or measuring wheel, sidewalk chalk

Focus

The world's biggest spider, the goliath bird-eater spider, has a pretty cool name. "Goliath" means giant. Explorers once saw one of these spiders eating a hummingbird and were very impressed. Despite their name, these *tarantulas* do not usually eat birds. They mostly eat insects, but occasionally they will eat slightly larger animals, like hummingbirds or frogs.

Present

❶ Consult Plan 13. On the playground (or appropriate indoor floor), draw a line that is 11 inches long. Using the illustration as a guide, have students draw the spider's head, body, and legs. Have students add fangs. The 11-inch line is about the size of a dinner plate or a small pizza. That is one big spider! (You might want to make two copies of Plan 13, cut out the larger images (they are actual size), and create a full-sized goliath bird-eater spider by taping the two halves together.)

❷ The goliath bird-eater spider lives in marshy areas, where it makes *burrows*. It does not use webs to catch its prey like many other spiders; instead, it waits for something to come along and then pounces on it, injecting *venom* into its new meal.

❸ Some people actually eat these spiders! People in places like Venezuela know how to prepare the spiders so that they're not poisonous. Ask students to talk about the craziest thing they've ever eaten. Did they like it, or would they never try it again?

──────────── *Vocabulary* ────────────
tarantula: a large, hairy spider
burrow: a hole dug by a small animal and used as a place to live
venom: a poisonous substance inside an animal

Conclude

Have students name their favorite animals, telling the class why they like these animals so much. Perhaps a few students will name the goliath bird-eater spider as their favorite after learning about it.

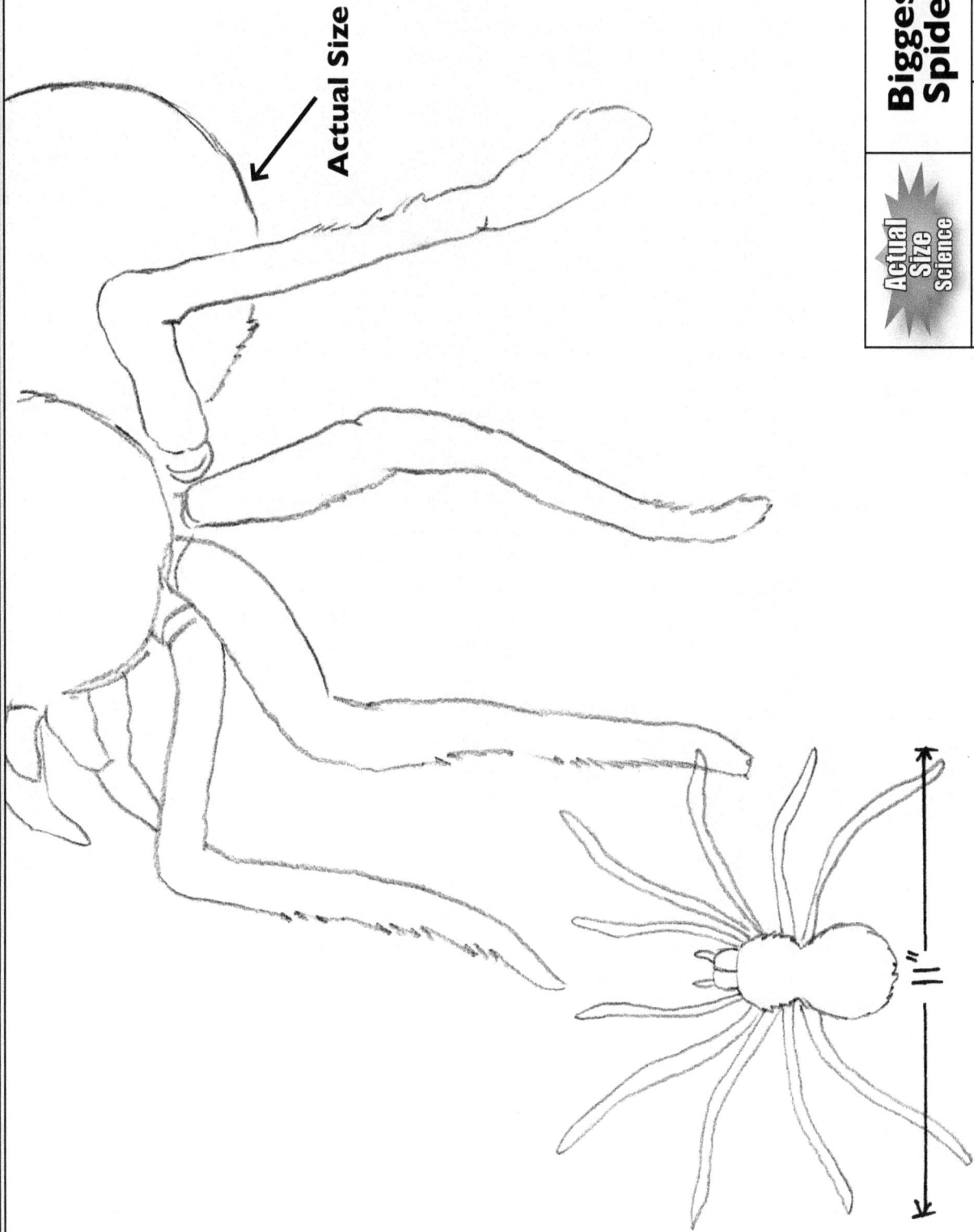

Actual Size

11"

Physical Science

The Grand Canyon

Students create a scale outline of the Grand Canyon in order to gain an understanding of just how massive the world's largest canyon is.

Prepare

- *Allow time:* approximately 1 hour for this activity
- *Gather materials:* Plan 14, ruler, measuring tape or measuring wheel, meter stick, sidewalk chalk or chalk line, scale figure

Focus

Ask students what some of the most famous natural places are. Not too down far the list will be the Grand Canyon. Explain to students what canyons are, and what the Grand Canyon is. Tell students that, for centuries, people have been awed by how huge the Grand Canyon is. Tell students that the Grand Canyon was carved by a river—the Colorado—in northern Arizona. Because it was carved by a twisting river, it is very curvy. If you stretched it out in a straight line, the Grand Canyon would be 277 miles long!

Present

❶ Consult Plan 14. Copy and cut out the scale figure. Show it to students, and explain that you will create a model of the Grand Canyon in proportion to this size person. Having a student hold the figure upright, place a meter stick vertically next to the figure. Explain that the Grand Canyon is over a mile deep at its deepest point, and that the meter stick represents the height of the canyon wall next to a person.

❷ Draw a line 227 feet long. Draw another that is 59 feet long at right angles to the first. Explain that, in addition to being very deep, the canyon is very wide. The Grand Canyon is up to 18 miles wide. Using the scale figure, point out that the 59-feet line represents this width. Tell students that people typically take three days to hike across the Grand Canyon.

❸ If the shorter line represents the width of the canyon, what to students think the longer line represents? If they infer the length—they're right...almost! Use the scale figure and tell them that the 227-foot-long line represents just one-fourth of the length of the Grand Canyon. To be to scale with the figure, the line would have to be four times as long as it is!

—————————— *Vocabulary* ——————————

grand: big or amazing
canyon: a deep valley with steep sides

Conclude

The Grand Canyon is between 5 and 6 million years old. This seems like a long time to us, but compared to many other geological formations, the Grand Canyon is very young. Some of the rocks at its base are around 2 billion years old. Discuss with students what the area must have looked like when the Colorado River was just beginning to carve the Grand Canyon.

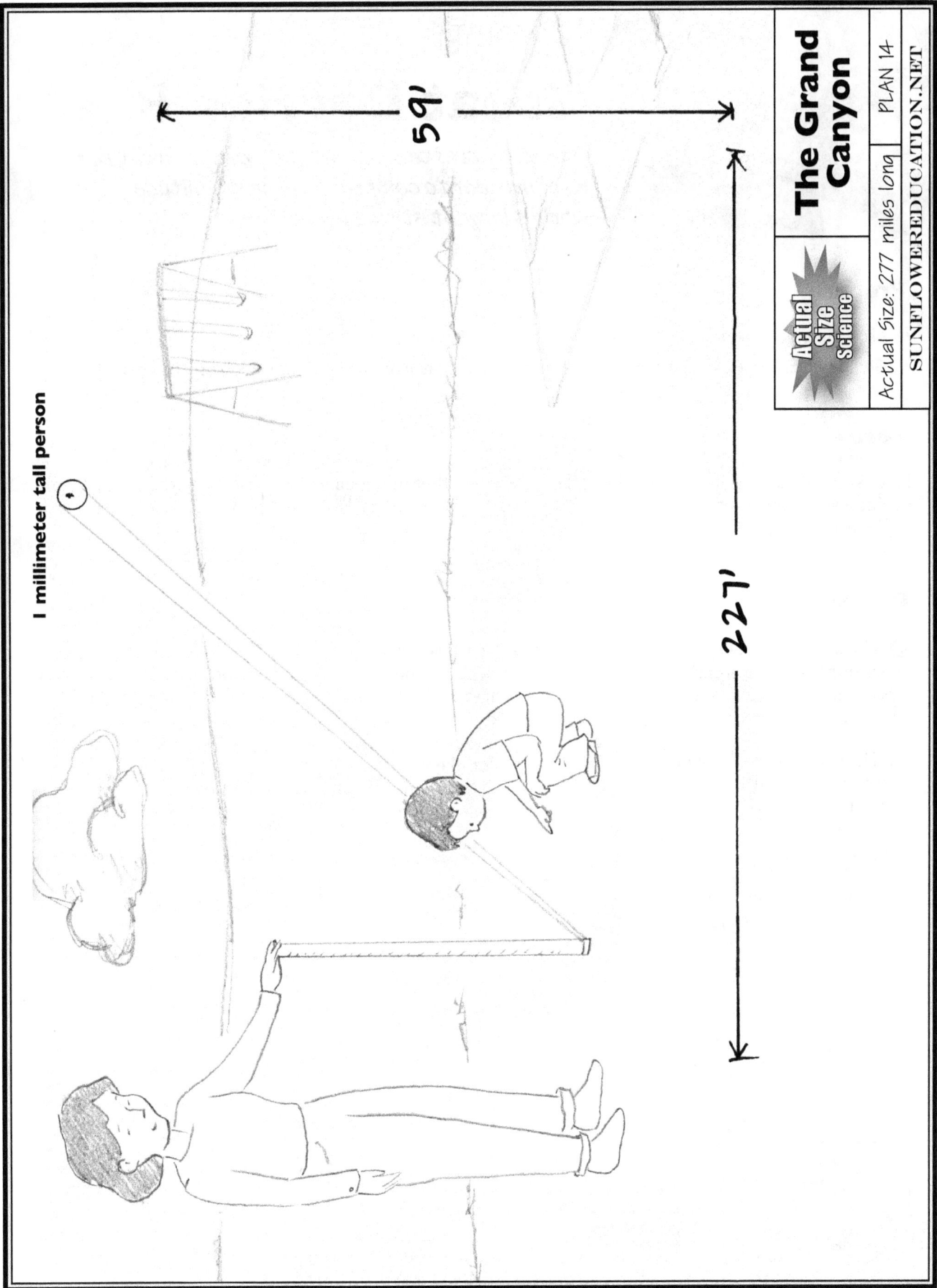

I millimeter tall person

59'

227'

The Grand Canyon

Actual Size Science

Actual Size: 277 miles long

PLAN 14-

SUNFLOWEREDUCATION.NET

Great Barrier Reef

Students create a scale outline of the Great Barrier Reef in order to comprehend the magnitude of the world's largest structure.

Prepare

- *Allow time:* approximately 45 minutes for this activity
- *Gather materials:* Plan 15, ruler, measuring tape or measuring wheel, sidewalk chalk or chalk line

Focus

Have students list the biggest buildings they've seen, either in person or in pictures. Skyscrapers, huge bridges, stadiums, even the Great Wall of China, are all much smaller than the world's largest structure: the Great Barrier Reef.

Present

❶ Consult Plan 15. On the playground (or appropriate indoor floor), measure out and draw a 124-foot line.

❷ Have a student lie down next to the line with a ruler. Tell students that the Great Barrier Reef is an amazing 1,240 miles long! In advance, pick out a well-known location approximately one mile from school and tell students that from school to that place is one mile. For us to be able to draw the Great Barrier Reef, every mile has to be only 1/10 of an inch long! It's that big! So imagine looking down on our drawing of the Great Barrier Reef. That's a lot like what it would look like from outer space. It would be impossible to see the student lying down next to it without a very powerful telescope.

❸ Ask students: can you guess how big the animals are that built the world's largest structure? They're tiny! The Great Barrier Reef is a *coral reef*. Coral reefs are built by animals called *polyps* that are only a few millimeters long. They live their whole lives on the coral reef in a tiny shell. At the end of their life, they leave their shell behind and it becomes a new part of the coral reef.

—————————————— Vocabulary ——————————————

coral reef: one of the massive underwater structures built by the remains of coral
coral: another name for polyps or their remains
polyp: a small underwater animal responsible for the creation of coral reefs

Conclude

Polyps are tiny. So how can they build something as big as the Great Barrier Reef? Part of the reason is how old the reef is. Polyps have been building up the Great Barrier Reef for around 30 million years, and they are still building. The other reason is just how many polyps work together to build the Great Barrier Reef. We can't count all of them—trillions and trillions—but just imagine how many tiny, little polyps it must have taken to create something so gigantic that you can see from space!

Coral Polyps

Actual Size

124'

Clown Fish

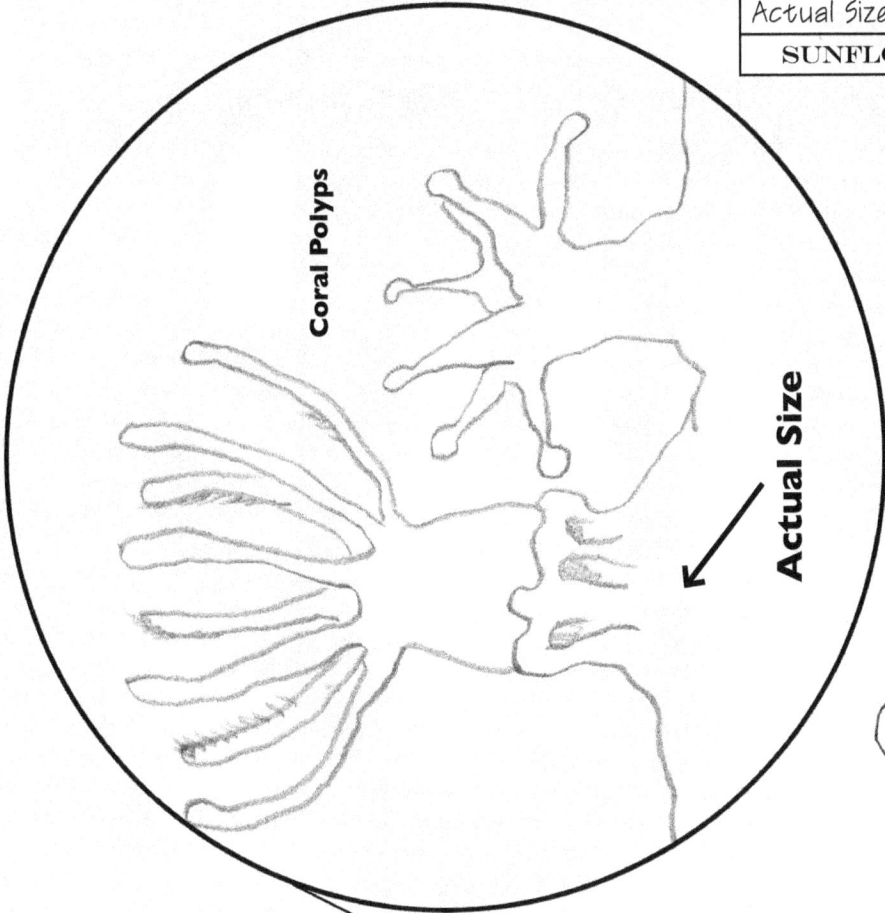

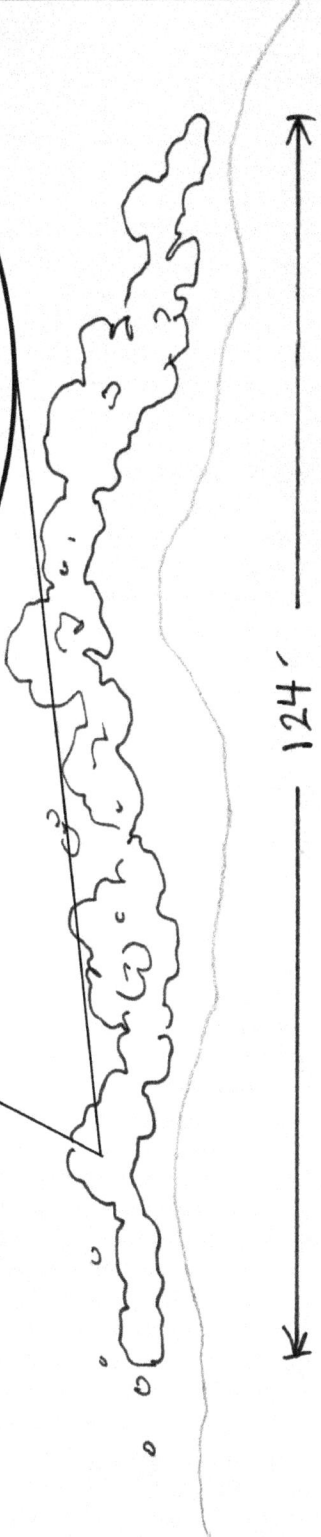

Meteor Crater (Barringer Crater)

Students create a scale outline of Meteor Crater (Barringer Crater) in order to better understand meteorites.

Prepare

- *Allow time:* approximately 45 minutes for this activity
- *Gather materials:* Plan 16, ruler, measuring tape or measuring wheel, sidewalk chalk, string, stake, $^1/_{10}$" figure

Focus

Discuss with students what is floating in space. There is much more than the stars, the planets, our satellites, and spacecraft. There are a lot of big rocks and chunks of metal floating around in space. When they come down to Earth we give them a special name. Any rock from space that makes it all the way to the ground is called a *meteorite*. Those that burn up in the air are called *meteors*.

Present

❶ Consult Plan 16. On the playground (or appropriate indoor floor), place a stake in the ground and tie a 38-foot piece of string to it (or have a student stand in one place and hold the string). Hold the end of the string and, keeping the string taught, draw a circle as you walk around the stake in the middle.

❷ If meteorites are really big, when they hit the ground they will form a *crater*. Meteor Crater is a very well preserved example of a crater in Arizona. Have a student lie down inside the outline of Meteor Crater with a ruler. Meteor Crater is 4,180 feet across! For us to be able to recreate it, we had to shrink it down. If a person were shrunk as much as our Meteor Crater they would be 1/10 of an inch tall!

❸ Why is Meteor Crater so well preserved? Because it's new. It's only about 50,000 years old. That would be a long time for someone to live, but for the age of the land on Earth, that is not long at all.

─────────── Vocabulary ───────────

meteorite: a space rock that makes it all the way to the ground
meteor: a space rock that burns up in Earth's atmosphere
crater: a hole in the ground, often created by a meteorite

Conclude

How heavy do you think something would have to be to make a hole as big as Meteor Crater? Scientists think that the meteorite that created Meteor Crater weighed 300,000 tons! That's more than 42,857 school buses! And to make that big of a crater, the meteorite had to be moving at 28,600 miles per hour!

1/10 " figure

76'

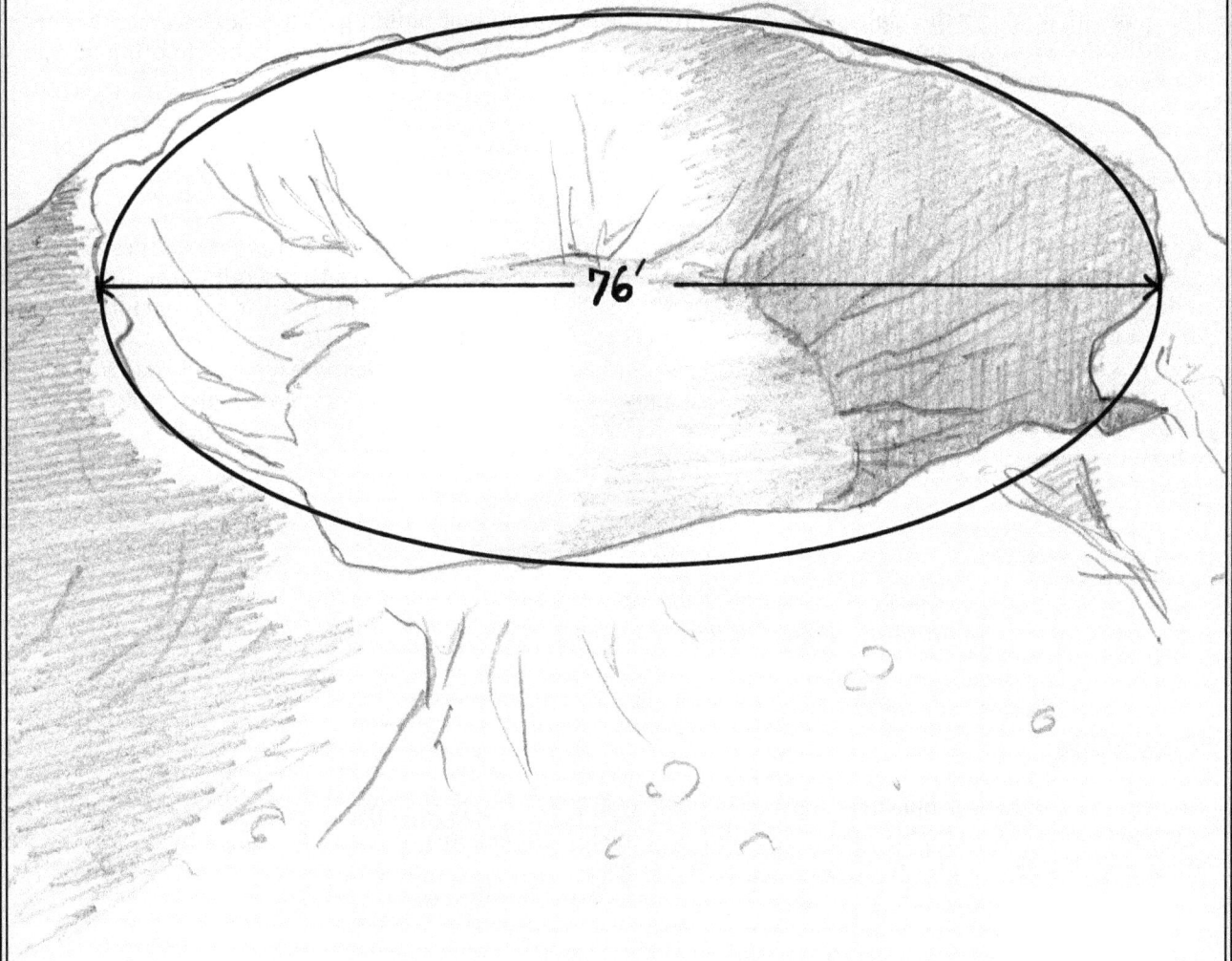

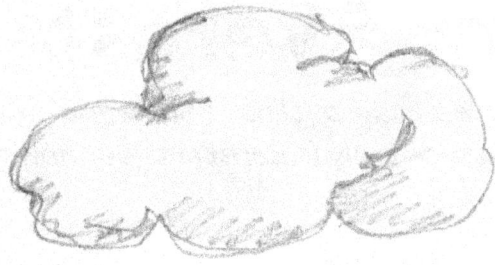

Mount Everest

Students create a scale outline of the world's tallest mountain in order to truly understand just how tall it is.

Prepare

- *Allow time:* approximately 45 minutes for this activity
- *Gather materials:* Plan 17, measuring tape or measuring wheel, sidewalk chalk or chalk line, ½" figure

Focus

Discuss with students the highest places they have been. Apartment buildings, skyscrapers, water towers, even the Rocky Mountains all fall beneath Mount Everest. At the very top, climbers need to bring *oxygen* tanks to be able to breathe because the air is so thin.

Present

❶ Consult Plan 17. On the playground (or appropriate indoor floor), measure out and draw a line that is 216 feet and 7 inches long. If time permits, let your students draw a large triangle at the top to give them a better visualization of this massive *mountain*.

❷ Cut out a copy of the ½ inch figure so your class can compare the awesome size of Mount Everest to a person. Explain that, in reality, Mount Everest soars 28,028 feet above sea level—that's more than five miles!

❸ Have students discuss all the things they would need to climb Mount Everest: warm clothes, tough shoes or boots, a tent, sleeping bags, a pick axe, ropes, matches, flashlights, a radio, oxygen for the top, et al.

—————————— *Vocabulary* ——————————
oxygen: a gas in the air that people need in order to live
mountain: a landform that rises higher than the surrounding area

Conclude

For a very long time, people have journeyed from around the world to climb the world's tallest mountain. They brave the steep climb, the extreme cold, and the low oxygen just to reach the top. Why do you think these people risk so much to climb to the top?

216' 7"

1/2" figure

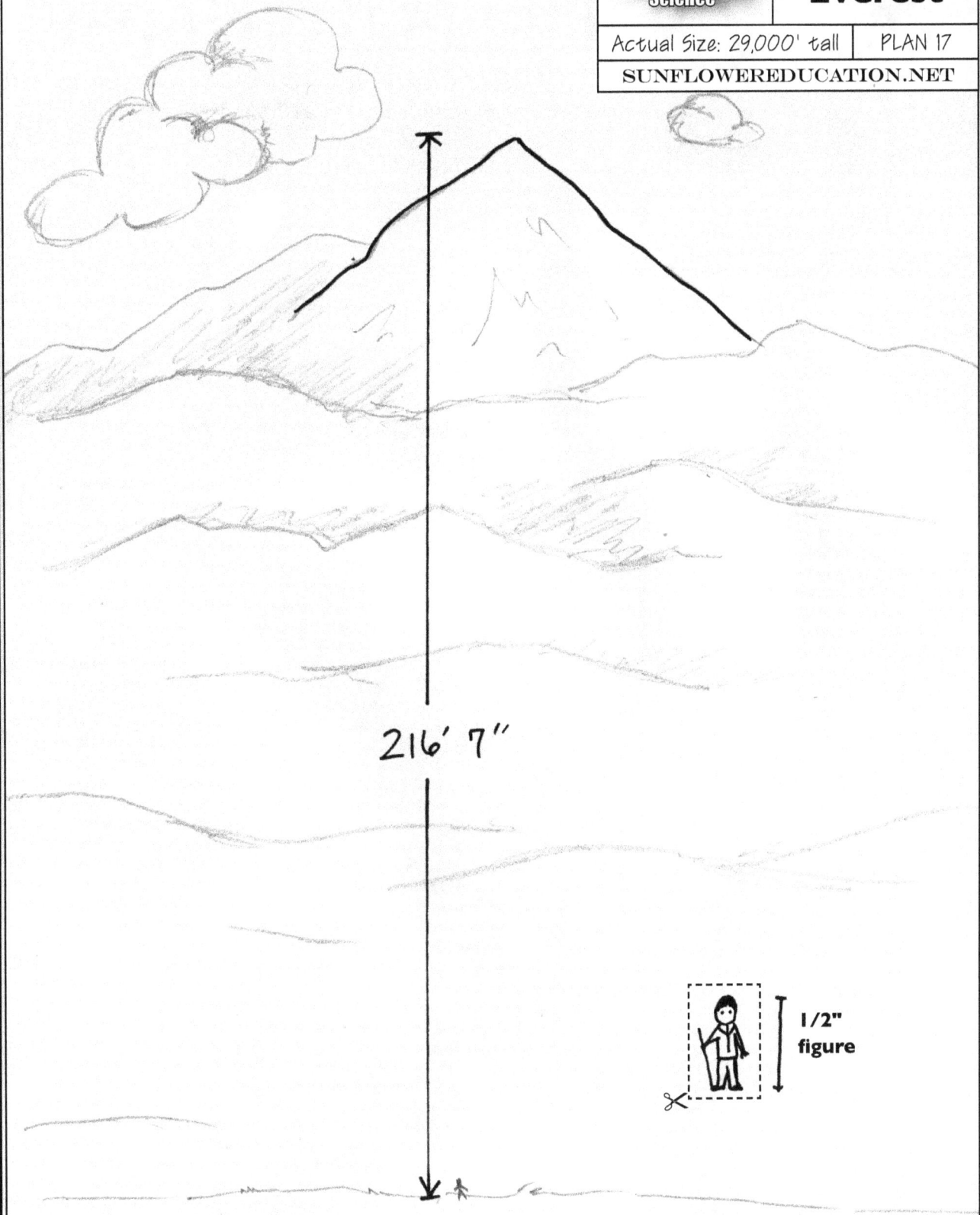

The Matterhorn

Students create a scale outline of the Matterhorn in order to appreciate the size of the world famous peak.

Prepare

- *Allow time:* approximately 45 minutes for this activity
- *Gather materials:* Plan 18, measuring tape or measuring wheel, sidewalk chalk or chalk line

Focus

Ask students what they imagine when they hear the word pyramid. Do they think of the great structures built in Egypt thousands of years ago, or of one of the many amazing step pyramids in the Americas? Before any of these existed, though, there was a natural pyramid in the Swiss Alps on the border of Switzerland and Italy: The Matterhorn.

Present

❶ Consult Plan 18. On the playground (or appropriate indoor floor), measure out and draw a line that is 263 feet long. Walk back 20 feet along this line and draw a 20 foot line perpendicular to the first and centered on the first line. Connect the ends of the shorter line to the near end of the long line. This is the pyramidal summit of the Matterhorn. Explain that the name Matterhorn is made from the German words for "meadow" and "peak."

❷ Have a student lie down at the base of our Matterhorn and hold a ruler. The Matterhorn soars 14,692 feet into the air. On our outline of the Matterhorn, the average person would be just 1/100th of an inch tall. Gaze up and appreciate just how huge the world's tallest pyramid is.

❸ How did a mountain get to be that shape? Scientists think that in the last million years, *glaciers,* or giant rivers of ice, moved along the European continent and helped to cut out many of the mountains there, including the Matterhorn! It's amazing to think that ice can change mountains.

—————————— *Vocabulary* ——————————

glacier: a huge river of ice that moves over land

Conclude

Discuss with students some of the other things glaciers helped to form: the Great Lakes, many beautiful valleys, icebergs, etc.

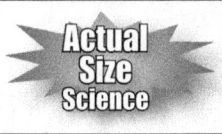

20'

20'

263'

© 2013 Sunflower Education

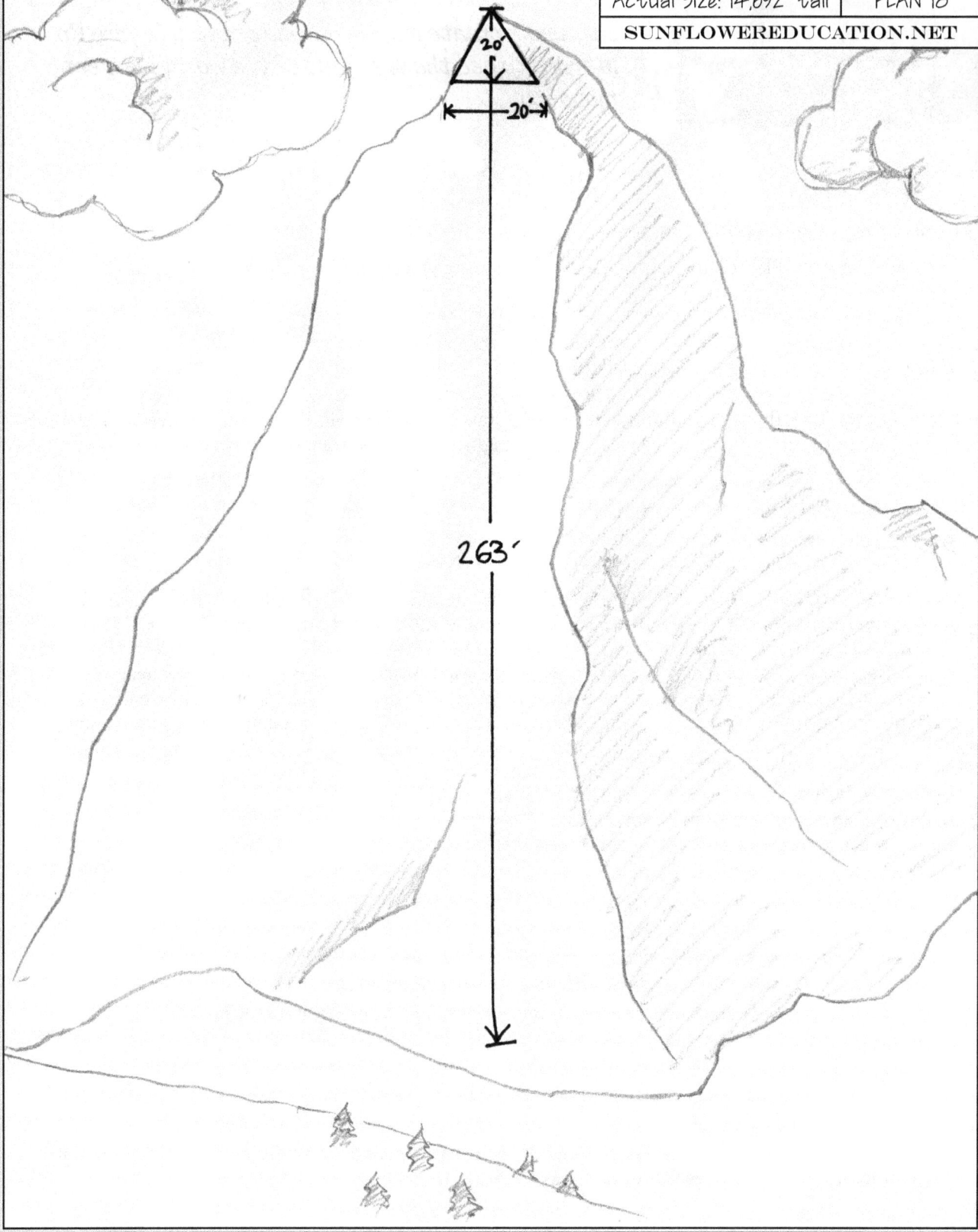

Uluru (Ayers Rock)

Students create a scale outline of Uluru (Ayers Rock) in order to see the vastness of the world's largest monolith.

Prepare

- *Allow time:* approximately 1 hour for this activity
- *Gather materials:* Plan 19, measuring tape or measuring wheel, sidewalk chalk or chalk line, 2" figure

Focus

Explain to students that a *monolith* is a huge stone standing all by itself. Uluru is a massive red monolith in the desert of central Australia. Have students imagine the biggest rock they have ever seen in preparation for this activity

Present

❶ Consult Plan 19. On the playground (or appropriate indoor floor), measure out and draw a line that is 170 feet long. This first line is the base. From the center of this line draw another line perpendicular to the first that is 34 feet long. This second line is the highest point of Uluru. Using the illustration as a guide, have students draw the rounded top and sides to complete the outline.

❷ Have a student lie down at the base of the outline and have them hold the cut out of the 2-inch figure for comparison. Explain that the actual size of Uluru is about 1,100 feet, or nearly three football fields, high. Prompt students to imagine the time it would take to explore all of Uluru.

❸ Uluru is a sacred site for Australia's *Aboriginal* people. There are many of their paintings here. The springs near Uluru have been used by people there for tens of thousands of years. Why might people consider such a rock sacred?

─────────── *Vocabulary* ───────────
monolith: a large stone all by itself
Aboriginal: a member of the earliest known people of Australia

Conclude

Uluru means "great pebble" in the language of the Aboriginal people of Australia. Encourage student discussion on why such a huge stone was called "pebble."

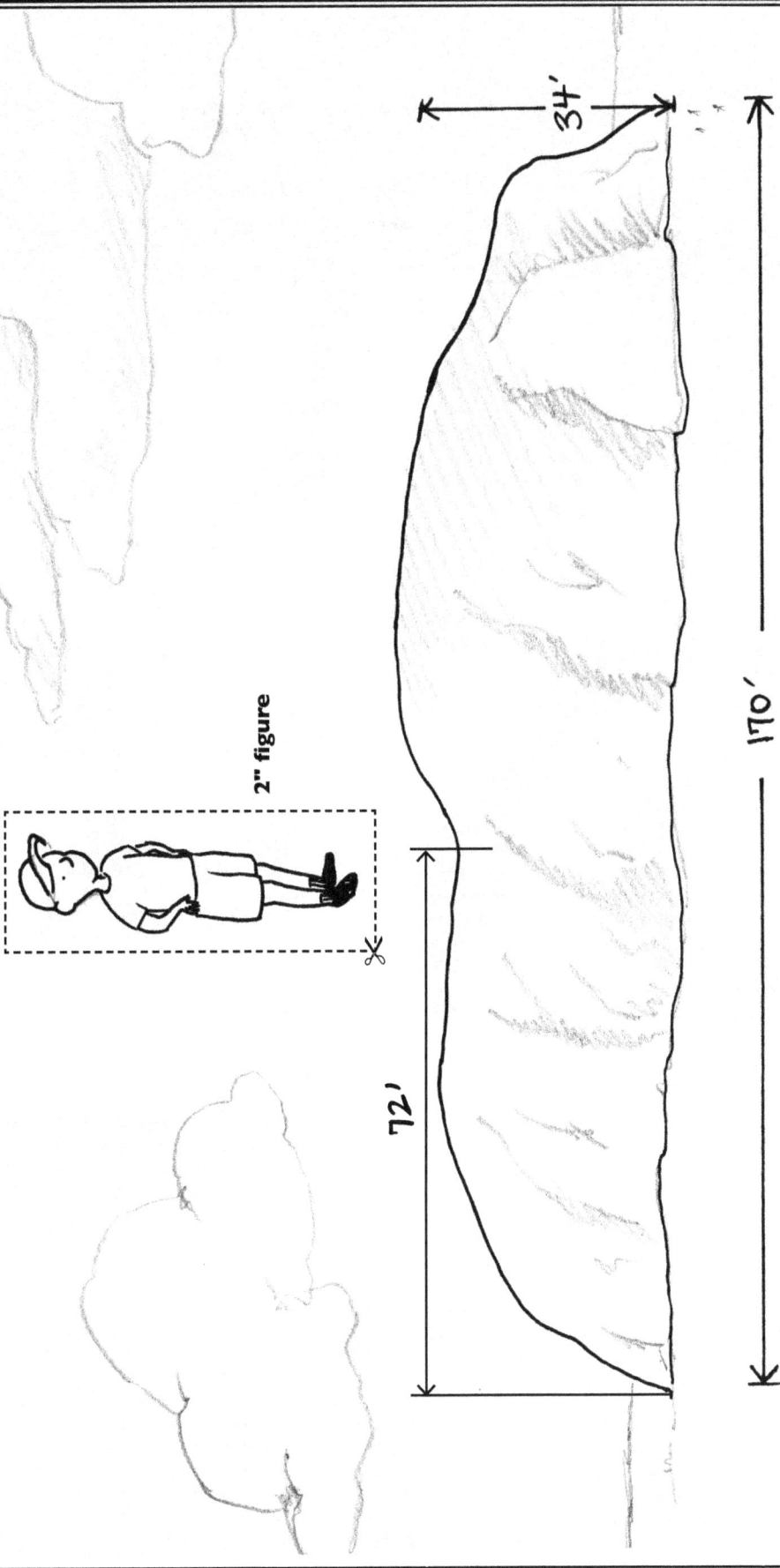

Uluru
(Ayers Rock)

Actual Size: 1,142' high	PLAN 19

SUNFLOWEREDUCATION.NET

Actual Size Science

34'

170'

2" figure

72'

Activity 20
Victoria Falls

Students create a scale outline of Victoria Falls in order to grasp the size of one of the world's widest waterfalls.

Prepare

- *Allow time:* approximately 45 minutes for this activity
- *Gather materials:* Plan 20, ruler, measuring tape or measuring wheel, sidewalk chalk or chalk line, carpenter's square, ⅓" figure

Focus

What are some ways we measure how big something is? How tall? How wide? How thick? How heavy? How deep? What do you imagine when you think of a big *waterfall?* If you are like most people, you imagine a very tall waterfall. But just like everything else, waterfalls have lots of ways of being big.

Present

❶ Consult Plan 20. On the playground (or appropriate indoor floor), measure out and draw a line that is 315 feet long. From the end of this line draw another line at a right angle that is 2 feet long. Then complete the rectangle, being very careful to keep the two 315-foot lines parallel to each other.

❷ The real Victoria Falls is 1 mile wide and 355 feet tall. To fit on the same scale as our outline of Victoria Falls, a person would have to be ⅓ of an inch tall. Have a student lie down at the base of the falls and hold up the ⅓-inch figure. So while it is really tall, the really big feature of Victoria Falls is how wide it is.

❸ Make sure students understand that the water coming down the falls would be falling in the 2-foot direction on our model. Encourage them to draw which way the water is flowing to ensure they understand.

——————————— Vocabulary ———————————
waterfall: where water in a stream falls over a drop in the terrain

Conclude

The people who live around the falls call them "Mosi-oa-Tunya", or "the smoke that thunders." Why do you think they would name this waterfall "the smoke that thunders?" Imagine what the falls must sound like to receive such a powerful name, and what the "smoke" might actually be (mist).

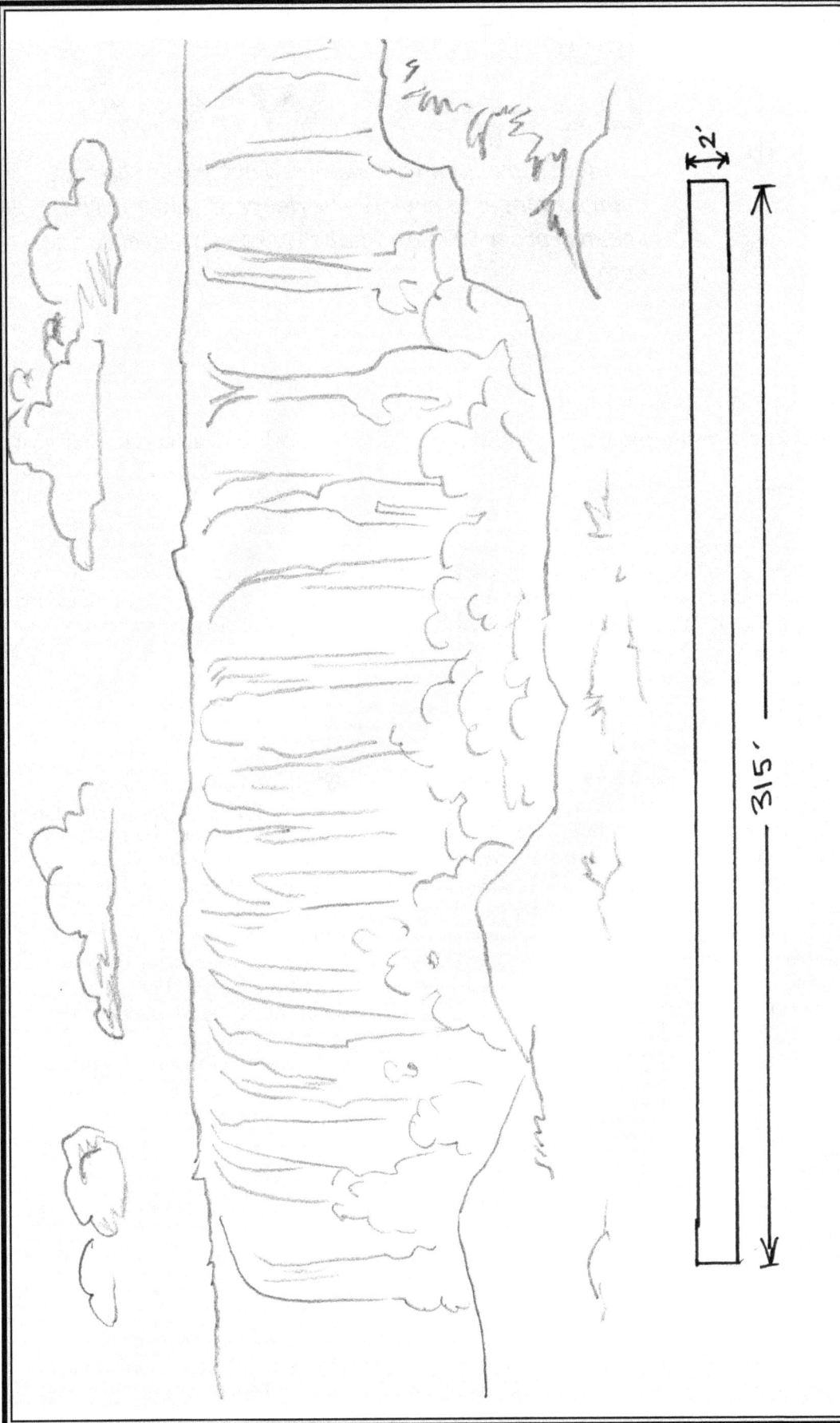

Victoria Falls

Actual Size Science

Actual Size: 1 mile wide   PLAN 20

SUNFLOWEREDUCATION.NET

315'

2'

1/3" figure

Deepest Water

Students create an actual-sized outline of the first manned vessel to explore the deepest water in the ocean in order to learn what it takes to travel to such depths.

Prepare

- *Allow time:* approximately 1 hour for this activity
- *Gather materials:* Plan 21, measuring tape or measuring wheel, string, stake, scale bathyscaphe, basketball goal

Focus

The world's deepest water, a spot in the Pacific Ocean known as the Challenger Deep, is 35, 994 feet (or 6. 82 miles) deep. In 1960, two men traveled to this depth in a *bathyscaphe,* a special ship designed for such deep water. These men, Jacques Piccard and Don Walsh, were the first people to ever travel this far down into the ocean.

Present

❶ Consult Plan 21. On the playground (or appropriate indoor floor), draw a line that is 60 feet long. Draw another, 12-foot line at a right angle to the first line. Complete the rectangle. Place a stake in the ground and tie a 5-foot piece of string to it (or have a student stand in one place and hold the string). Hold the end of the string and, keeping the string taught, draw a circle as you walk around the stake in the middle.

❷ This is an actual-size outline of the bathyscaphe *Trieste.* The larger upper area served as a float to return the vehicle to the surface (ballast was used to sink it to the ocean floor). The smaller circular area was the sphere where the two men travelled.

❸ In preparation for this activity, photocopy the following page and cut out the small square made by dotted lines. This is a bathyscaphe that has been drawn to scale. Take this cut-out bathyscaphe and place it underneath a basketball goal, which should be about 10 feet tall. This is a scale model of the *Trieste* at Challenger Deep, with the basketball rim representing the ocean's surface.

—————————— *Vocabulary* ——————————
bathyscaphe: a ship that can travel far down into the ocean

Conclude

Pick out a place from school that is between 6 to 7 miles away. Now ask your students to imagine what it would be like if that distance was all under water. Imagine having all that water sitting on top of you! Have students sit in the circular part of the outline. What would it be like to ride in a bathyscaphe to the bottom of the sea?

Deepest Water

Actual Size: 6.82 miles deep | PLAN 21

SUNFLOWEREDUCATION.NET

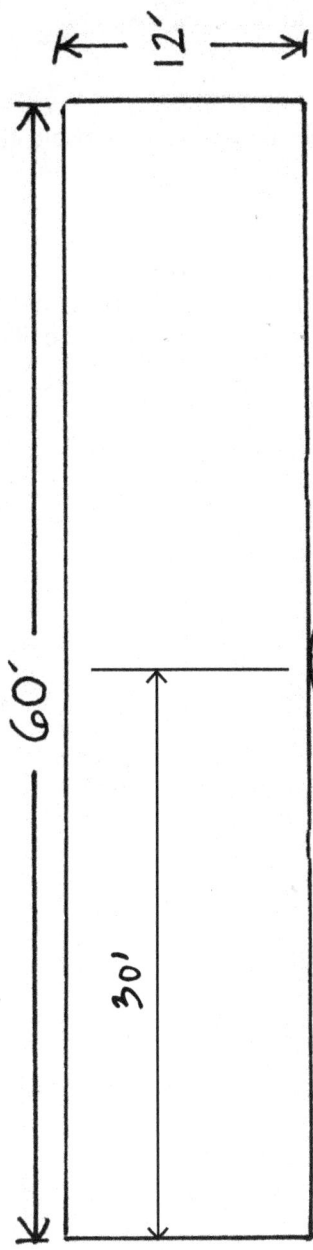

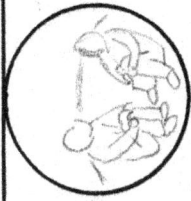

12'

60'

30'

10'

Amazon River

Students create a scale outline of the Amazon River in order to grasp the size of the world's longest river.

Prepare

- *Allow time:* approximately 1 hour for this activity
- *Gather materials:* Plan 22, ruler, measuring stick or measuring wheel, sidewalk chalk, string

Focus

Ask students to think about the last time they went to a river. Maybe there is one in your town with which students are familiar. Now tell them to imagine what that river would be like if it were 4,000 miles long! That is how long the Amazon River is.

Present

❶ Consult Plan 22. In preparation for this activity, measure out and cut two strings that are each 88 feet long. On the playground (or appropriate indoor floor), draw a 6-inch line. Have 2 volunteer students hold the two strings. One of the two students should place the ends of the pieces of string on the ends of the 6-inch line and hold the strings tightly. Have the other student hold the other ends of the strings and walk in the opposite direction, trying to take a winding path.

❷ Explain to students that each foot on the strings represents 45 miles! The 6-inch line that students drew is not drawn to scale; for most of the Amazon River's course, it's about 6 miles wide, but it is 90 miles (two inches at this scale) wide at its *mouth!* There's a lot of variety in this river's width. The largest ship ever built—about a quarter mile long—would be only 1/16" long!

❸ The Amazon River is sometimes called "the River Sea." Ask students why people would call it by this name. The river is so big that it reminds people of the ocean.

--- Vocabulary ---

biodiversity: variety of living things
mouth: the part of a river that empties into another body of water

Conclude

The world's longest river flows through the world's largest rainforest, the Amazon Rainforest. The Amazon Rainforest is known for its amazing *biodiversity* because of all the different plants and animals who live there. One in ten of the world's species live in the Amazon rainforest!

88´

6"

✂ ┈┈
1/16" ship

Actual
Size
Science

**Amazon
River**

Actual Size: ~4,000 miles long | PLAN 22

SUNFLOWEREDUCATION.NET

Activity 23
Clouds

Students create scale outlines of different clouds and their relative heights in the sky in order to understand clouds and their distance above ground.

Prepare

- *Allow time:* approximately 1½ hours for this activity
- *Gather materials:* Plan 23, measuring stick or measuring wheel, sidewalk chalk or chalk line

Focus

Have you ever spent an afternoon looking at shapes in the *clouds?* Were they fluffy balls of cotton, wispy horse-tails, the flat surface of a pond, or maybe a giant mountain moving in the distance?

Present

❶ Consult Plan 23. On the playground (or appropriate indoor floor), mark off a 20-foot by 20-foot square. Choose one side to be the "ground" and have a volunteer student draw a tree or building so the ground is obvious. Draw two horizontal lines, splitting the "sky" into three sections. Label these sections "low clouds," "middle clouds," and "high clouds." Divide the students into three groups. Assign each group a type of cloud to draw. In the lower left portion of the sky, draw flat stratus clouds. In the upper left portion of the sky, draw wispy cirrus clouds. In the bottom right portion of the sky draw fluffy cumulus clouds. After discussing all three types of clouds, have the entire class build up the cumulus clouds to form cumulonimbus cloud (See Plan 23). Use the scale skyscraper and airplane to help students visualize the size and height of clouds.

❷ Clouds are made up of tiny *droplets* of water or tiny ice crystals that are so small and light that they fall very slowly. They fall so slowly that the tiniest bit of wind will push them back up in the air. Rain forms when enough of these tiny droplets of water join together and form a raindrop, which is heavy enough to fall.

❸ Cumulonimbus clouds are also called "thunderheads." Discuss with your students why this is. Cumulonimbus clouds are the clouds that typically produce thunderstorms. This lesson presents a good opportunity to introduce students to weather safety.

Vocabulary
---

cloud: *a mass of droplets of water or ice in the air that you can see*

droplet: *a tiny drop*

Conclude

We have seen that clouds can occupy all different spaces in the sky, from way up high to very low. But what happens when a cloud gets so low that it rests on the ground? You might have seen this on a cold morning on the way to school. We call it fog. Have you ever imagined what it must be like inside of a cloud? Now you know! It is wet! After all, clouds are just little drops of water floating in the air.

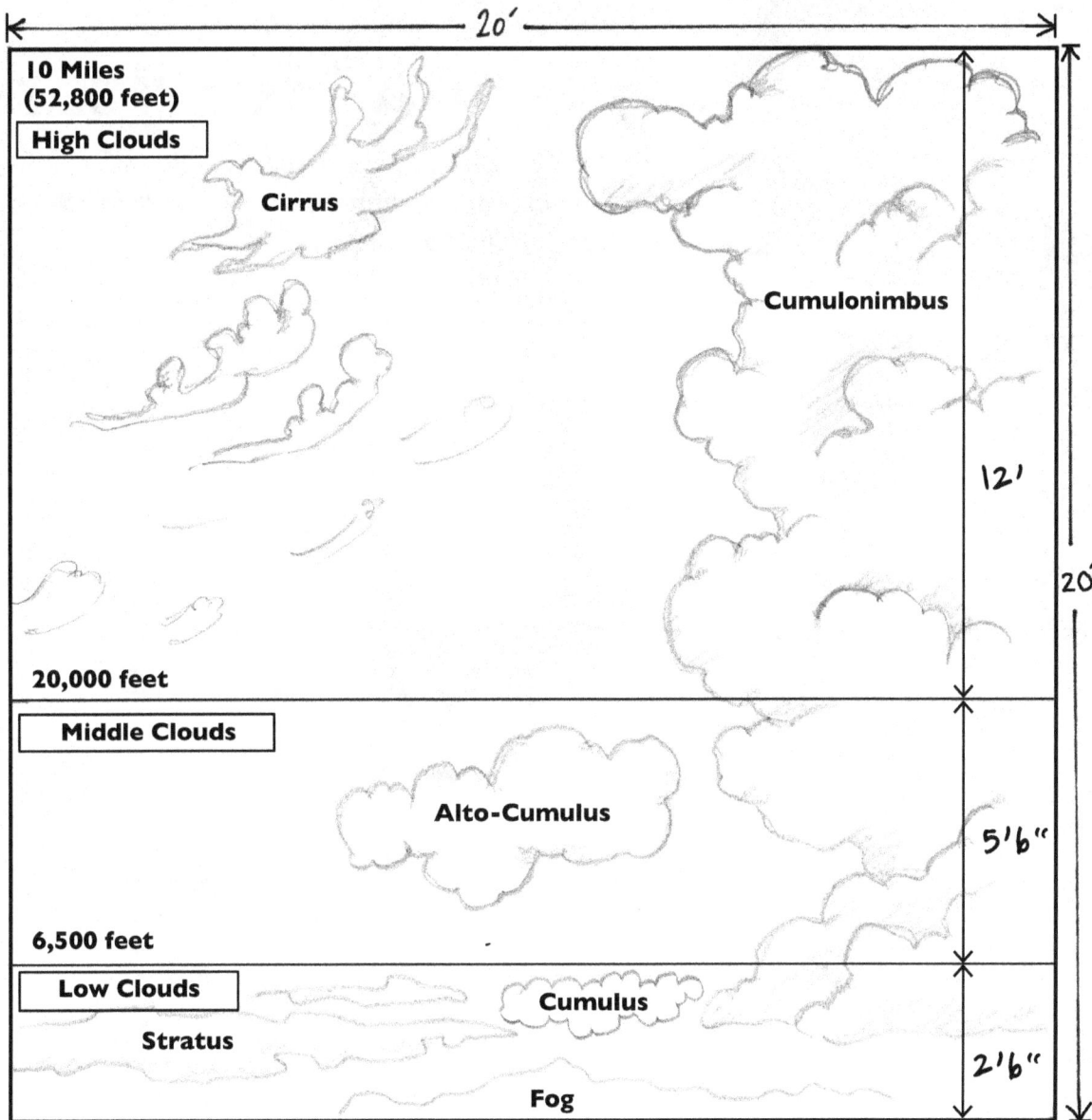

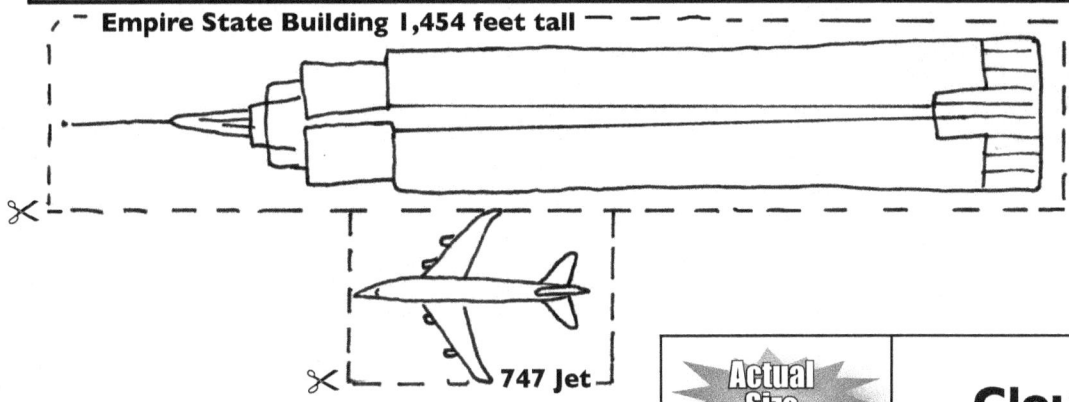

10 Miles (52,800 feet)

High Clouds

Cirrus

Cumulonimbus

12'

20'

20,000 feet

Middle Clouds

Alto-Cumulus

5'6"

6,500 feet

Low Clouds

Cumulus

Stratus

2'6"

Fog

Empire State Building 1,454 feet tall

747 Jet

Actual Size Science

Clouds

Actual Size: 6,500'-52,800' high | PLAN 23

SUNFLOWEREDUCATION.NET

© 2013 Sunflower Education

20'

Eye of a Hurricane

Students create a scale outline of the eye of a hurricane in order to appreciate the enormous size of these powerful storms.

Prepare

- *Allow time:* approximately 1 hour for this activity
- *Gather materials:* Plan 24, measuring tape or measuring wheel, sidewalk chalk, string, stake, 1" Orion airplane

Focus

A hurricane is a massive circular storm. Did you know that the center of a hurricane can be the calmest part of it? The center, or *eye, of a hurricane* is usually circular and is 20 to 40 miles in diameter. Strangely enough, the area around the eye, called the *eyewall,* is one of the worst parts of the storm.

Present

❶ Consult Plan 24. On the playground (or appropriate indoor floor), draw a circle 90 feet in diameter. This represents a 20-mile diameter eye. Copy Plan 24 and cut out the airplane, which is drawn to scale. Explain to students that the eye they drew would be 20 miles wide in real life, and the eyewall would be 6 ½ miles tall! That would be 30-feet high in the model, or abut the height of a three-story building. Even more impressive: the diameter of hurricanes can reach 1,000 miles. In the model, the hurricane would reach almost ½ a mile in all directions.

❷ The airplane on the next page is called an Orion. It is one inch in our drawing, but it is 100 feet long and 100 feet wide in real life. "Hurricane Hunters," people who work for the United States government, fly these planes into the very eye of the hurricane! They use scientific tools to learn about the hurricane, so that every one on land will know what to expect. Have students fly the Orion through the middle of the "eye" that you drew. Have them imagine being in a plane at the very middle of a huge storm.

--- Vocabulary ---

eye of a hurricane: the calm area at the middle of the storm
eyewall: the stormy border of the hurricane's eye
evaporate: when water turns into vapor

Conclude

So how do hurricanes happen? A hurricane is a storm that gathers heat from warm ocean water. It continues to *evaporate* warm water from the ocean, and this fuels it even more. By the time it reaches land, it features strong winds and tons of rain, and can cause large waves in the ocean.

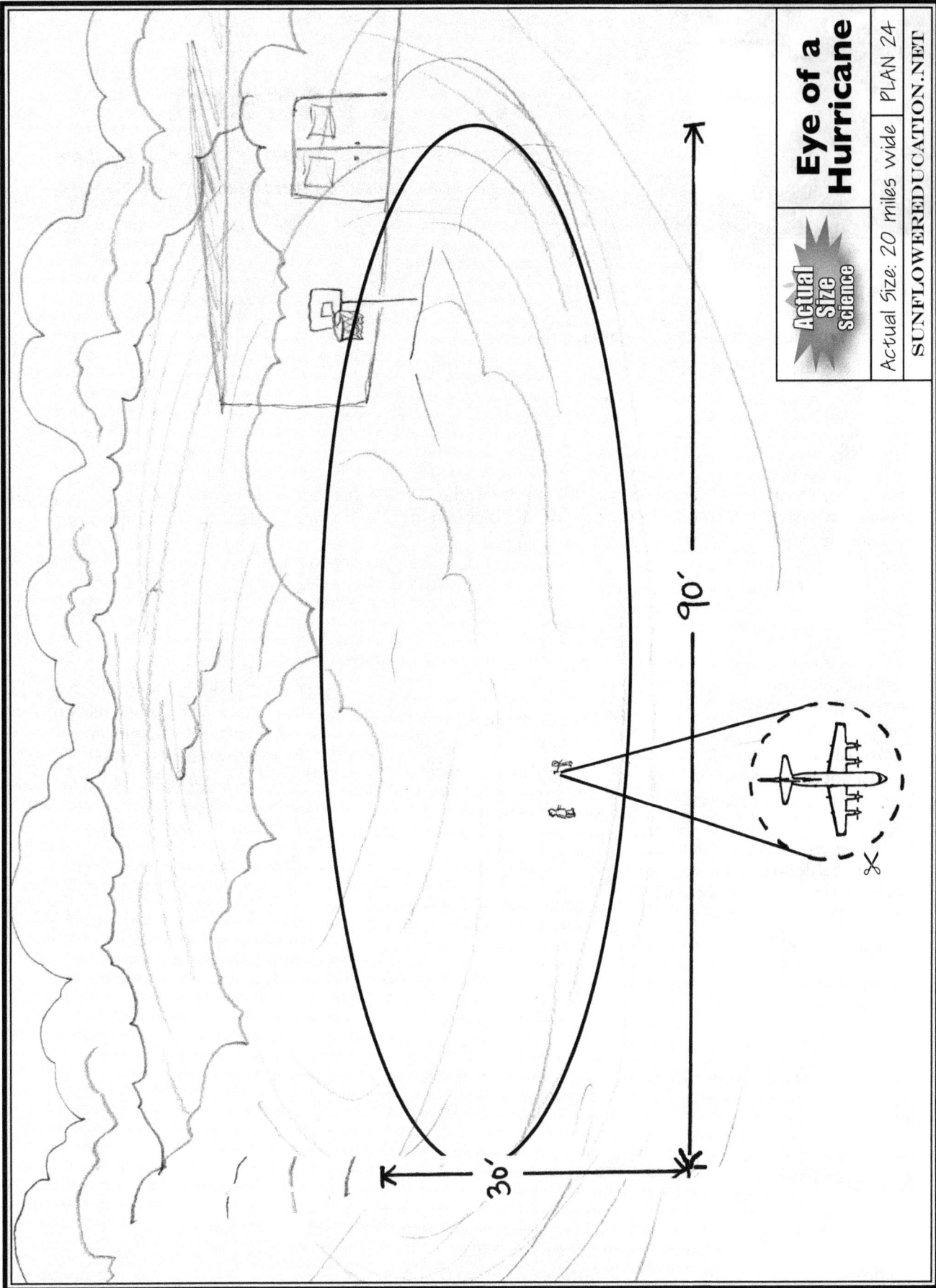

Eye of a
Hurricane

Actual
Size
Science

Actual Size: 20 miles wide | PLAN 24
SUNFLOWEREDUCATION.NET

90'

30'

Solar System

Students create a scale model of the solar system in order to gain an accurate understanding of its vast size.

Prepare

- *Allow time:* approximately 1½ hours for this activity
- *Gather materials:* Plan 25, measuring tape or measuring wheel, sidewalk chalk, sheets of paper, pen

Focus

How far can you see on a clear day? 93 million miles, the average distance from here to the Sun! How huge is the solar system? We often see pictures of the solar system (like the one on this page) with the *planets* and Sun much closer together than they actually are.

Present

❶ Consult Plan 25. Draw and label the Sun and the planets, each on their own page. The Sun should be a circle 3.8 inches across. Mercury should be as small a dot as you can make with a pen in the center of the page. Venus should be a dot just barely larger than Mercury. The Earth should be a dot the same size as Venus. Mars should be about as small a dot as Mercury. Jupiter should be a circle .39 inches across. Saturn should be a circle .33 inches across. Uranus should be a tiny circle .14 inches across.

Neptune should be the same size as Uranus.

❷ Have students look at the sheets and the size of all the objects in their to-scale solar system. Discuss how this differs from other pictures of the solar system they have seen. Discuss how far apart the sheets need to placed to be to scale. Take them to the playground or football field. Have a student hold the Sun on one end of the space and begin measuring in a straight line from there. Have a student stand

with a planet as you reach each of them. Follow the distances on Plan 25 (to be practical, stop at Saturn). Tell students about the *astronomical unit (AU)*. Have students estimate various distance between planets and the Sun in AUs.

❸ Have students look at the other sheets from where they are positioned. How many of the other planets can they see? What kinds of tools would they need to use to see the other planets?

—————————————— Vocabulary ——————————————

astronomical unit (AU): the distance between the Sun and the Earth (about 93 million miles)
planet: a spherical ball of rock and/or gas that orbits a star

Conclude

This lesson is a good opportunity to talk about thousands, millions, and billions using the actual distances between the planets and the Sun as examples. The Earth is 7,926 miles across. Mercury is 36,000,000 miles from the Sun. And Pluto is 3,666,000,000 miles from the Sun.

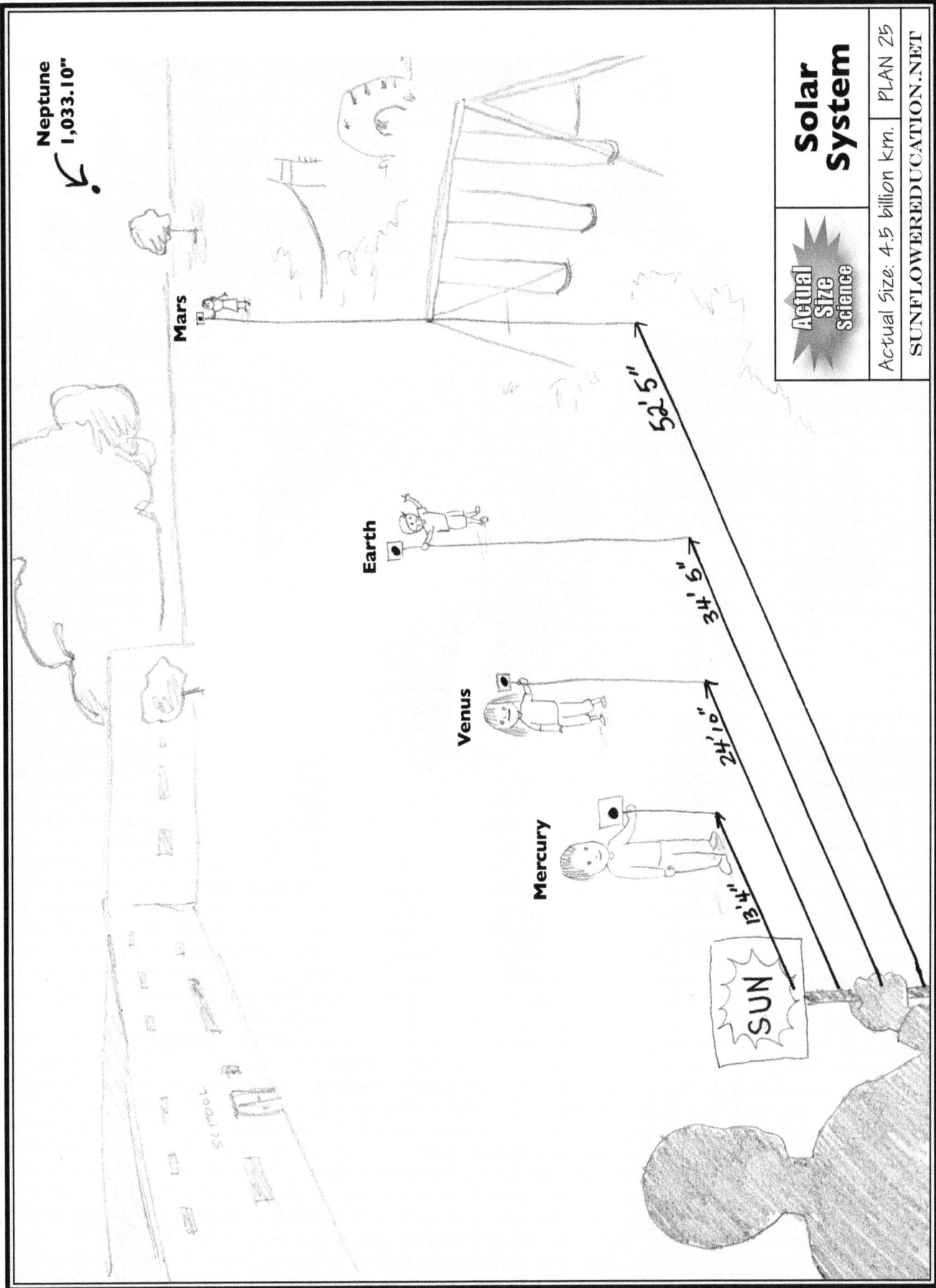

Neptune
1,033.10"

Mars

Earth

Venus

Mercury

52'5"

34'5"

24'10"

13'4"

SUN

Solar System

Actual Size Science

Actual Size: 4.5 billion km. | PLAN 25

SUNFLOWEREDUCATION.NET

Technology

Activity 26
First Aircraft

Students create a scale of the world's first aircraft that carried people in order to better understand the history of flight.

Prepare

- *Allow time:* approximately 1 hour for this activity
- *Gather materials:* Plan 26, measuring stick or measuring wheel, sidewalk chalk, markers, pencil, paper

Focus

So a sheep, a duck, and a rooster walked onto a hot air balloon... no, it's not a joke! These animals flew in one of the first hot air balloons, which was *invented* in the late 1700s by the Montgolfier brothers (Jacques Etienne and Joseph Michel) in France. They wanted to show the French king that their new invention worked. On November 21, 1783, two Frenchmen made the first human free flight in history, soaring over Paris in a Montgolfier balloon for about 25 minutes.

Present

❶ Consult Plan 26. On the playground (or appropriate indoor floor), draw a line that is 74 feet long. At the top of this line, draw a perpendicular, 48-foot line. Using the illustration as a guide, have students draw in a picture of the hot air balloon.

❷ Did you know that hot air actually weighs a little bit less than cold air, making the hot air rise above cooler air? This very simple scientific idea is actually what makes a hot air balloon work. The hot air balloon invented by the Montgolfier brothers used air heated by fire. Once that air got hot, up it went, and the balloon went with it.

❸ Have your class imagine that they are flying over their town in a hot air balloon. What would it be like to be in a hot air balloon? What would they see on their trip? How would they describe it to their friends and families?

❹ The Montgolfier balloon was decorated with golden colored pictures of the sun and stars. Let your students decorate their hot air balloon in any way they like.

——————— *Vocabulary* ———————

invent: to make something that is completely new

Conclude

It must be pretty cool to invent something. Ask students to create an invention of their own. Have them draw these inventions on a piece of paper and describe them to their classmates. What would they name their invention, what does it do, and how did they get the idea for it? Encourage creative effort.

© 2013 Sunflower Education

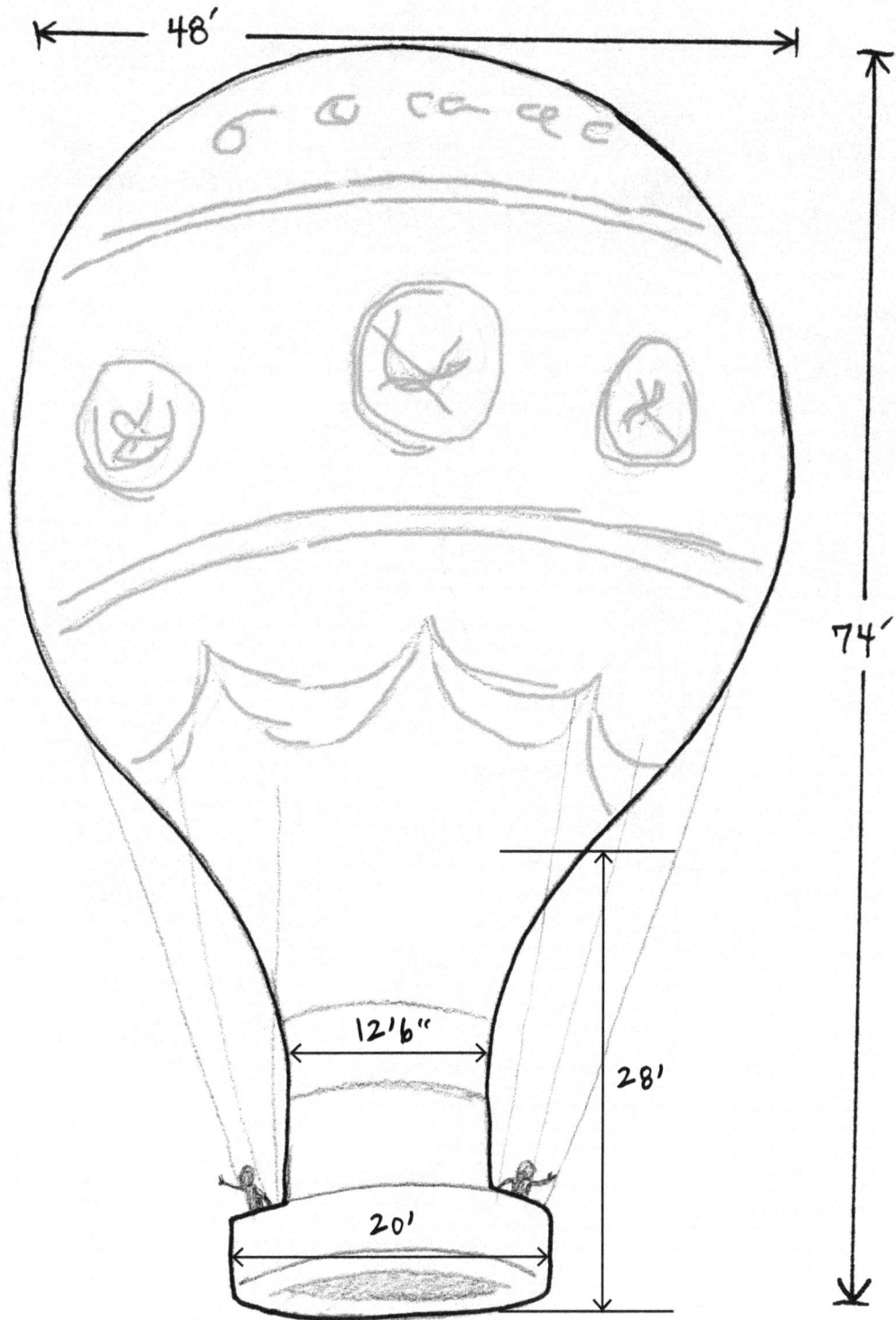

← 48' →

74'

28'

12'6"

20'

Actual Size Science

First Aircraft

Actual Size: 48' x 74' | PLAN 26

SUNFLOWEREDUCATION.NET

Early Computer

Students create an actual-sized outline of ENIAC, the first working digital computer, in order to see how far computers have come.

Prepare

- *Allow time:* approximately 1 hour for this activity
- *Gather materials:* Plan 27, measuring stick or measuring wheel, sidewalk chalk or chalk string

Focus

When was the last time you used a *computer?* Explain to students that modern computers are used by lots of different people for different purposes. Explain to them that not long ago, computers were huge machines that cost so much to build that only governments or large companies could afford them.

Present

❶ Consult Plan 27. On the playground (or appropriate indoor floor), reproduce the inverted U-shape. Tell students that this was how big ENIAC was. It was eight feet tall.

❷ ENIAC stands for Electronic Numerical Integrator And Computer. There were other computers before ENIAC, but ENIAC was the first *functional* computer to perform all of its calculations electronically.

❸ ENIAC was first used to perform tests for the hydrogen bomb. To perform these calculations, ENIAC had to be given instructions. Today, we can simply type on a keyboard or download instructions into a computer, but ENIAC received instructions through huge stacks of cards with holes punched in them. It is much easier now!

————————————— Vocabulary —————————————

computer: a machine, usually electronic, that can take in, store, and make calculations with information
digital: electronic
functional: working

Conclude

ENIAC was a huge leap forward for computers. As the first fully *digital* computer, ENIAC worked 1,000 times faster than the computer before it! This is the biggest jump yet in computer power! But computers are much, much more powerful today. Today's typical laptop is more than 1,000 times more powerful than ENIAC!

20'

34'

2'

8'

Actual Size Science

Early Computer

| Actual Size: 34' x 20' | PLAN 27 |

Activity 28
Sputnik

Students create a to-scale outline of Sputnik, the first artificial satellite to orbit Earth, in order to gain an appreciation of the history of space exploration.

Prepare

- *Allow time:* approximately 45 minutes for this activity
- *Gather materials:* Plan 28, measuring tape or measuring wheel, sidewalk chalk, string, stake, globe

Focus

What is the name of the first *satellite* to *orbit* the Earth? The moon! But the first *artificial* satellite was called Sputnik, launched in 1957. Discuss with students the significance of Sputnik: how it inspired the imaginations of countless people, led to the creation of NASA, and eventually led to the first successful landing on the moon.

Present

❶ Consult Plan 28. On the playground (or appropriate indoor floor), place a stake in the ground and tie an 11.4-inch piece of string to it. Draw a circle. From the top and bottom of the circle, draw a line sweeping back in the same direction 9 feet and 4 inches. These lines represent the antennae and should be at approximately 35° (See Plan 28).

❷ Ask your students what satellites are used for today: GPS, communications, and the study of the Earth and space. Discuss with students how far satellite technology has come since 1957. Sputnik contained a radio that is simple compared to modern radios and transmitted beeps at regular intervals on two frequencies.

❸ Talk with students about how high above the Earth satellites like Sputnik fly. Sputnik orbited the Earth every 90 minutes at about 200 miles above the surface of the Earth. 200 miles seems far, but lets look at that distance next to the Earth. The Earth is 7,926 miles in diameter. This means that on a 12-inch globe, Sputnik's height in orbit would be about .3 inches above the globe (about the width of a fingernail).

―――――――――――― *Vocabulary* ――――――――――――

satellite: an object in orbit
orbit: the path of an object going around a star, planet, or other object in space
artificial: made by people, not naturally occurring

Conclude

On November 3, 1957, one month after Sputnik 1 was launched, Sputnik 2 carried the first living passenger into space. Her name was Laika, and she was a dog. Discuss with students how quickly space exploration advanced and significant milestones in space exploration.

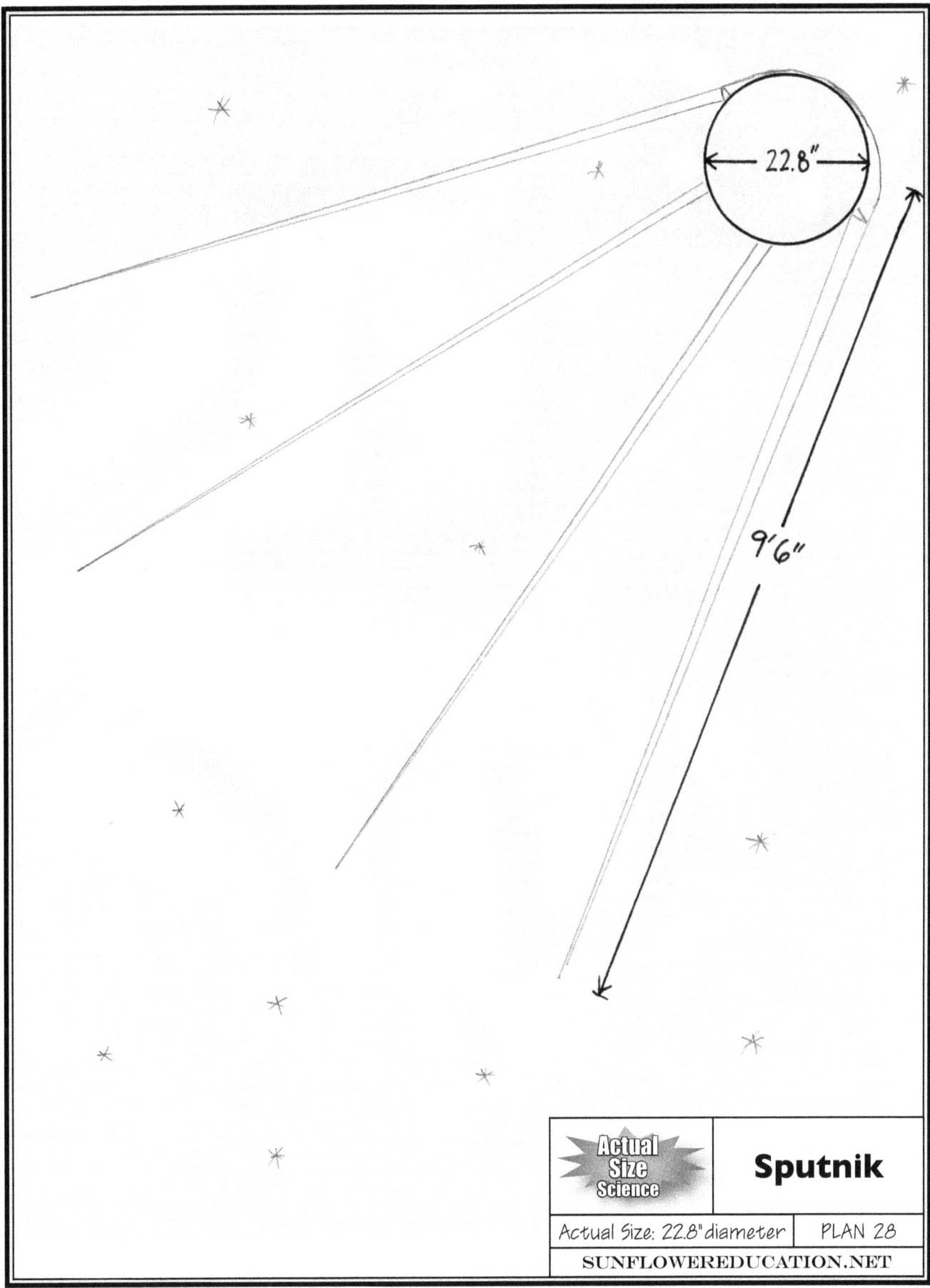

22.8"

9'6"

Actual Size Science

Sputnik

Actual Size: 22.8"diameter | PLAN 28

SUNFLOWEREDUCATION.NET

Mercury Capsule

Students create a full-scale outline of the Mercury Capsule in order to understand the conditions the first American astronaut dealt with.

Prepare

- *Allow time:* approximately 45 minutes for this activity
- *Gather materials:* Plan 29, measuring stick or measuring wheel, sidewalk chalk, string, stake

Focus

Space has fascinated people for a very long time. Shortly after World War II, the *Space Race* between America and the Soviet Union began. This race had several legs: putting an object in orbit, putting a person in space, and finally landing on the moon. The *Mercury* Capsules were part of the United States' efforts to put people into space and to orbit the Earth.

Present

❶ Consult Plan 29. On the playground (or appropriate indoor floor), place a stake in the ground and tie a 3-foot 1-inch piece of string to it (or have a student stand in one place and hold the string). Hold the end of the string and, keeping the string taught, draw a circle as you walk around the stake in the middle. Follow Plan 29 to sketch out the rest of the capsule.

❷ The first American *in* space was Alan Shepard. He flew Mercury 3, which was also called Freedom 7. The first American to *orbit* the Earth was John Glenn, who flew Mercury 6, also called Friendship 7. Both of these men were American heroes, but when they accomplished their goals the Soviet Union had already done these things. It wasn't until December 1968, when three American astronauts orbited the moon, that the United States passed the Soviet Union in the Space Race.

❸ Have students spend time in the Mercury Capsule outline. Point out that with all of the scientific instruments and controls inside the capsule, the astronauts who flew them only had enough space to sit in one position. This meant that John Glenn had to sit in the same cramped position for almost 5 hours during his trip into space, the three orbits around Earth, and the return trip. Encourage students to imagine what that must have been like.

—————————————— Vocabulary ——————————————

Space Race: the competition between the USA and the USSR to beat each other in space exploration
Mercury: a Roman messenger god known for his speed

Conclude

Discuss with students how far we have come in space flight since the days of the Mercury Capsules. We landed on the moon, built the International Space Station, and have countless satellites in orbit. The Mercury Capsules and the Space Race provide a good introduction for a discussion of the Cold War and the history of the second half of the 20th century.

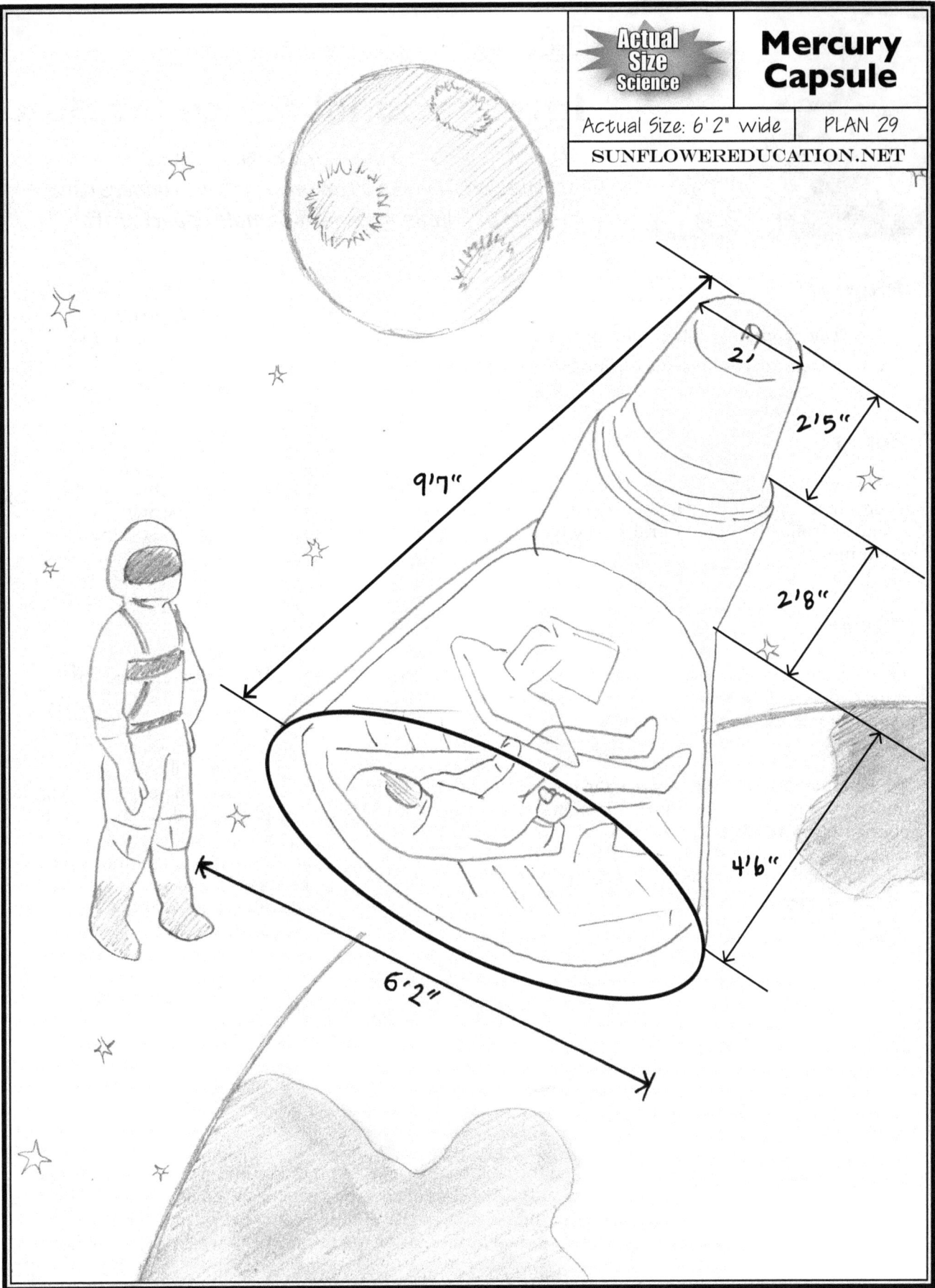

2'

2'5"

9'7"

2'8"

4'6"

6'2"

International Space Station

Students create a life-sized outline of the International Space Station in order to understand the size of humanity's most complex spacecraft.

Prepare

- *Allow time:* approximately 1 hour for this activity
- *Gather materials:* Plan 30, measuring tape or measuring wheel, sidewalk chalk, string

Focus

Discuss with students where people have lived throughout history. Have students list all the extreme environments people have lived, like the desert or rain forest. In the *International* Space Station, scientists from all over the world are studying the effects of living in space, one of the most extreme environments.

Present

❶ Consult Plan 30. Consider using a local athletic (football) field to create the life-sized diagram.

❷ Point out that the majority of this space is made up of the solar panels (the outboard rectangles), which provide power to the International Space Station. To gain an idea of the space astronauts actually live in, focus students' attention on the central section.

❸ Bring students inside of the inner section. Have them imagine what it would be like to spend weeks inside this space along with a lot of scientific equipment. What would they like? What would they dislike?

Scientists in the International Space Station are studying lots of things to learn more about how people can live in space and on other planets, like the effects of *microgravity* on people, plants, fire, germs, et al. If time permits, encourage students to draw the scientific equipment they would be spending their days with in the International Space Station.

———————————————— Vocabulary ————————————————

international: involving two or more countries
microgravity: very low gravity; the reason astronauts float in space

Conclude

Explain to students that the creation of the International Space Station was a united effort. 16 countries worked together to assemble this Space Station. The lives of everyone who has lived in or visited the International Space Station depend on the parts from all these different countries fitting together perfectly and working together. The International Space Station is a testament to what people can do when we work together.

Actual
Size
Science

**Space
Station**

Actual Size: 356' x 240' | PLAN 30

SUNFLOWEREDUCATION.NET

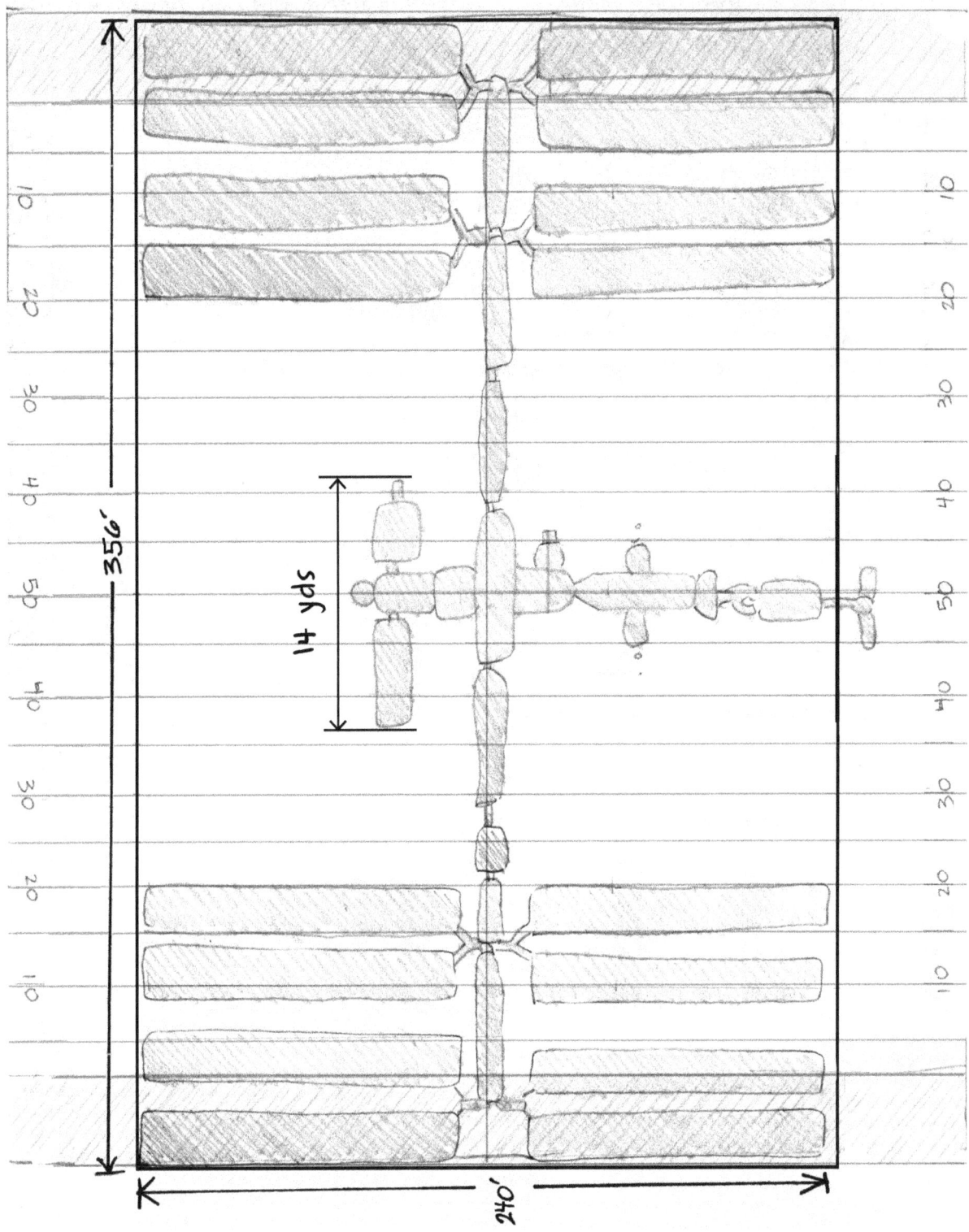

356'

240'

14 yds

Hubble Space Telescope

Students create a full-scale outline of the Hubble Space Telescope in order to appreciate this modern marvel.

Prepare

- *Allow time:* approximately 1½ hours for this activity
- *Gather materials:* Plan 31, measuring stick or measuring wheel (use meters), sidewalk chalk

Focus

The Hubble Space Telescope is no ordinary telescope. It orbits the earth at a rate of 5 miles per second; at this rate, the telescope could travel across the United States in 10 minutes. The Hubble Telescope is also an amazing scientific tool—it has helped scientists figure out how old the universe is!

Present

❶ Consult Plan 31. On the playground (or appropriate indoor floor), draw a line that is 13.2 meters long. Draw another, 4.2-meter line at a right angle and at one end of the first line. Centered within these lines, draw a rectangle that is 3.2 meters by 9.2 meters. Draw another rectangle beneath it that is 4.2 meters by 4 meters. Draw a line from each side of the first, larger rectangle, connecting it to what represents the two *solar panels,* which are 2.6 meters by 7.1 meters.

❷ A *telescope* is a device that can make things that are really far away look much closer than they really are. The Hubble Space Telescope, like many telescopes used on Earth, uses mirrors to collect light. Once all that light has been collected, the Hubble Space Telescope takes pictures to send back to Earth. These pictures are much more accurate than ones taken by telescopes on Earth. This is because images from Earth-bound telescopes are changed by the *atmosphere,* the layer of gases that surrounds our planet. The Hubble Space Telescope, though, is located beyond the Earth's atmosphere.

———————————————— Vocabulary ————————————————

solar panel: a flat device that collects sunlight and turns it into energy
telescope: a tool that helps people see far away by collecting and focusing light
atmosphere: a layer of gases that surrounds the earth

Conclude

Discuss with your students why the Hubble Space Telescope is so important to science. Before this telescope, scientists could come up with ideas about the universe, but they couldn't actually see what was happening. Now they can see parts of the universe, almost as if they were actually there!

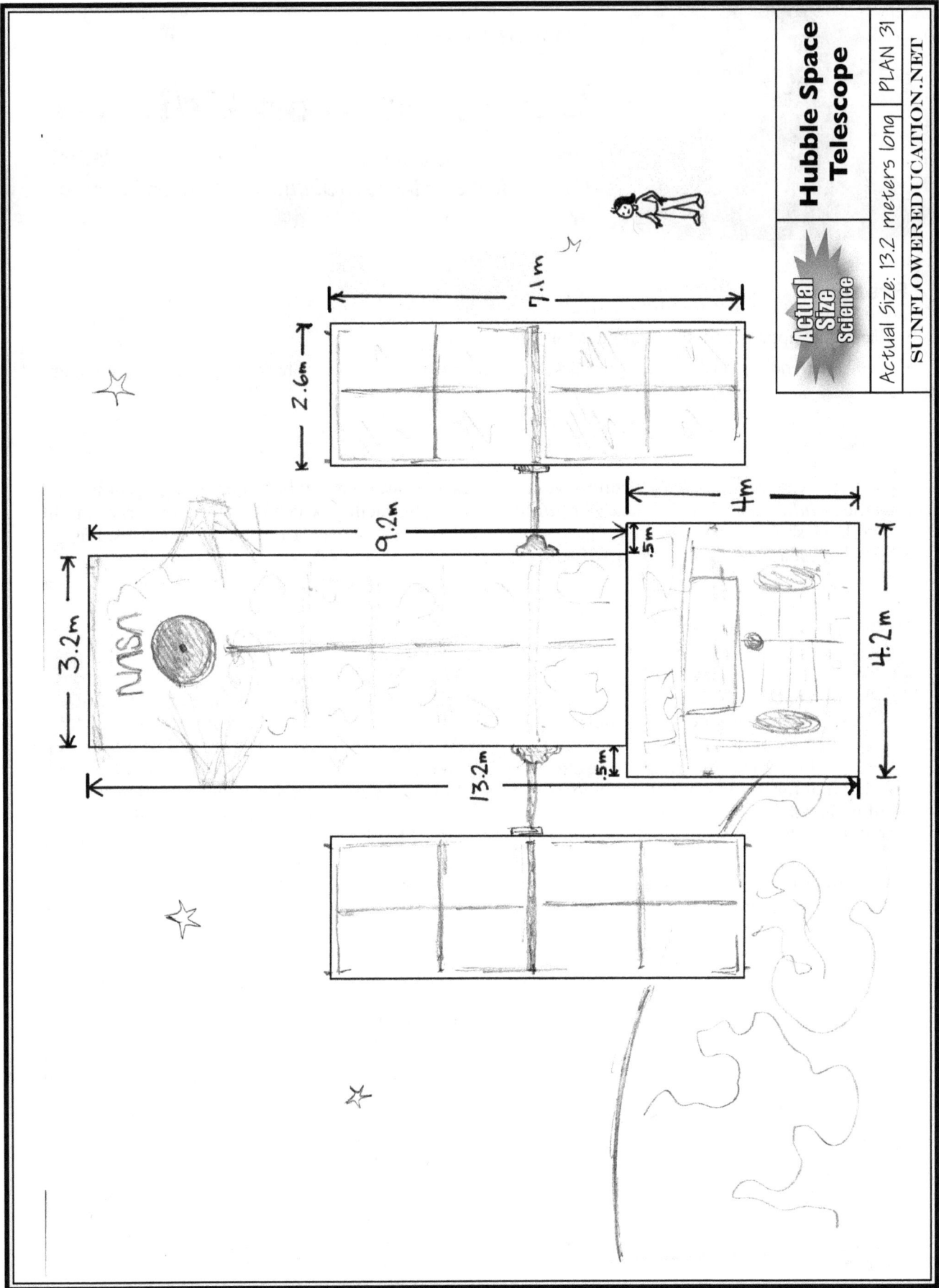

7.1 m

2.6 m

9.2 m

3.2 m

4m

.5 m

.5 m

4.2 m

13.2 m

NASA

Large Hadron Collider

Students create a scale outline of the Large Hadron Collider in order to learn about this new addition to science.

Prepare

- *Allow time:* approximately 45 minutes for this activity
- *Gather materials:* Plan 32, measuring stick or measuring wheel, sidewalk chalk, string, stake, 2 mm figure

Focus

If you have ever crashed into someone in your school's hallway, then you have something in common with the *colliding particles* in the Large *Hadron* Collider. This facility, which is 574 feet underground in Switzerland, shoots particle beams at each other to help scientists answer important questions. It is the world's largest and highest-energy particle accelerator.

Present

❶ Consult Plan 32. Photocopy the Plan and cut out the 2 mm person. On the playground (or appropriate indoor floor), place a stake and tie a 4 1/2-foot piece of string to it (or have a student stand in one place and hold the string). Hold the end of the string and, keeping the string taught, draw a circle as you walk around the stake in the middle. The diameter of the Large Hadron Collider is actually 9 kilometers, not 9 meters. Place the 2 mm cut-out person in the middle of the circle to give students an idea of how big the Hadron Collider is.

❷ So why is the Large Hadron Collider important? In the past, scientists discovered that the science we use to measure ordinary things does not work well when we use it for really small or really big things. Many scientists are still confused about this. They hope that the Large Hadron Collider will help them understand the smallest types of matter, which are the building blocks of the things we see everyday.

———————————— Vocabulary ————————————

collide: to hit something while moving
particle: a really small piece of matter
hadron: a type of particle
data: a list of the outcomes of many experiments; information

Conclude

The Large Hadron Collider can run experiments searching for a type of particle, the Higgs particle, every few hours. In March 2013, scientists collected enough *data* to tentatively confirm the existence of the Higgs particle. Discuss with students why it is so important to collect a lot of data when you're doing an experiment.

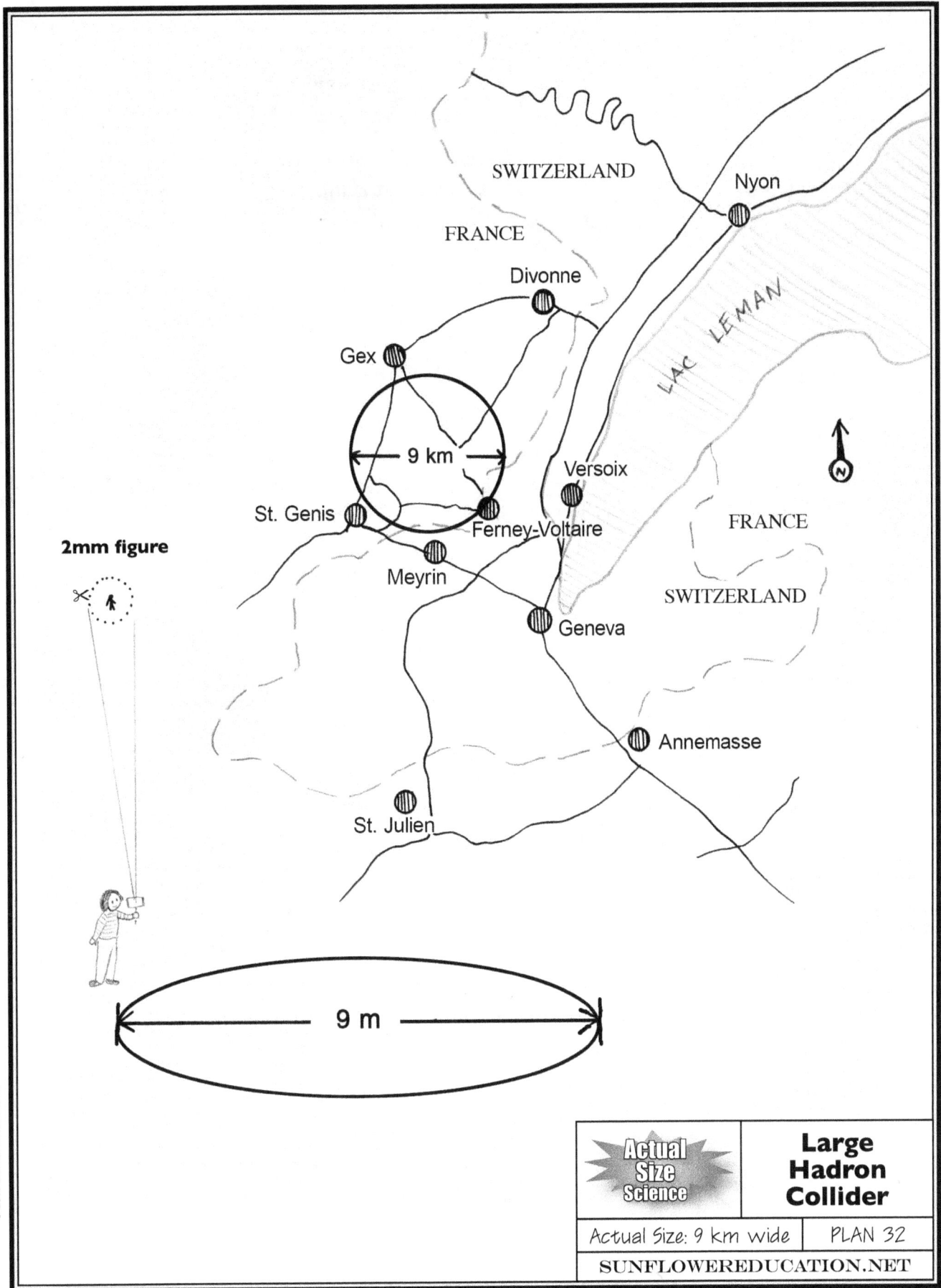

SWITZERLAND

FRANCE

Nyon

Divonne

LAC LÉMAN

Gex

9 km

Versoix

St. Genis

FRANCE

Ferney-Voltaire

2mm figure

Meyrin

SWITZERLAND

Geneva

Annemasse

St. Julien

9 m

Actual Size Science

Large Hadron Collider

Actual Size: 9 km wide | PLAN 32

SUNFLOWEREDUCATION.NET

Activity 33
Tallest Dam

Students use scale figures to visualize the height of the world's tallest dam.

Prepare

- *Allow time:* approximately 30 minutes for this activity
- *Gather materials:* Plan 33, measuring stick or measuring wheel, sidewalk chalk, scale family

Focus

Ask students to guess how many dams there are worldwide. There are about 36,000 dams in the world! There is one very special dam, though, in Tajikistan, in Eastern Europe. The Nurek dam is the world's tallest dam, standing an astonishing 984 feet tall!

Present

❶ Consult Plan 33. Copy the Plan and cut out the scale family. Find a four-story building (or use the 4th floor of a taller building); this building (or floor) will be around 41 feet tall. Place the cut-out family next to it. Prompt your students to imagine that they are looking up at Nurek Dam—it would be that tall!

❷ Ask your students if they know why dams are constructed. When a dam is built, it makes some of the river water higher and some lower. The dam *generates*, or creates, electricity and helps prevent the river from flooding. Dams also provide a source of drinking water.

❸ The Nurek Dam is next to a power plant which can supply 98% of Tajikistan's electricity! That is almost all of the electricity needed by this country of nearly 8 million people. So how does the dam create this electricity? When water falls from the higher level to the lower one, it flows over a bunch of *turbines,* which spin and make electricity.

———————————————— Vocabulary ————————————————
generate: to make something
turbine: a machine with blades that spin when water flows over it, producing electricity

Conclude

Did you know that beavers build dams, too? These animals are good swimmers, but they aren't very fast on land, so they had to come up with a way to hide from their predators. They make dams, which create places where the water is deeper. That means there's more space where they can hang out without worrying about predators.

984'

Fold

Actual
Size
Science

**Tallest
Dam**

Actual Size: 984' tall | PLAN 33

SUNFLOWEREDUCATION.NET

Deepwater Drilling

Students create a to-scale model of deepwater drilling on a classroom wall in order to appreciate the importance of oil in today's world.

Prepare

- *Allow time:* approximately 45 minutes for this activity
- *Gather materials:* Plan 34, measuring stick or measuring wheel, sidewalk chalk, tape, scale ship

Focus

What is oil? It is actually made up of the remains of plants and animals that lived millions of years ago. This is why it is called a *"fossil fuel."* Companies *drill* very far under the ground or beneath the ocean floor in order to get to it.

Present

1 Consult Plan 34. Make a photocopy of the ship. In real life, this drillship would be 835 feet long. Cut it out and tape it to an appropriate wall 15 feet off the ground. Measuring from the ship downwards, mark off 5 feet and draw a horizontal line through this point. This represents the ocean floor, which would actually be about 10,000 feet beneath the ship. Draw a line between the ship and the "ocean floor," and extend it down to the actual floor. This will be 10 feet in your model, but its actual size would be 20,000 feet beneath the ocean floor! This is how deep beneath the ocean floor that companies can drill for oil.

2 Ask students why people would go so far beneath the ocean floor to get oil. Explain to students that many people around the world use oil and gas to fuel their cars and create electricity. Because of this, companies can make a lot of money selling it, which means that they can afford to drill 20,000 feet beneath the ocean floor.

--- Vocabulary ---

fossil fuel: fuel that is formed from the remains of plants and animals
drill: a tool that can be used to make holes in something
pollute: to put harmful substances in the environment

Conclude

Deepwater drilling is a pretty impressive way to use technology, but it also creates problems. Discuss with students that deepwater drilling can go wrong and create oil spills, which harm animals and people in several ways. Oil and gas also *pollute* the air around us.

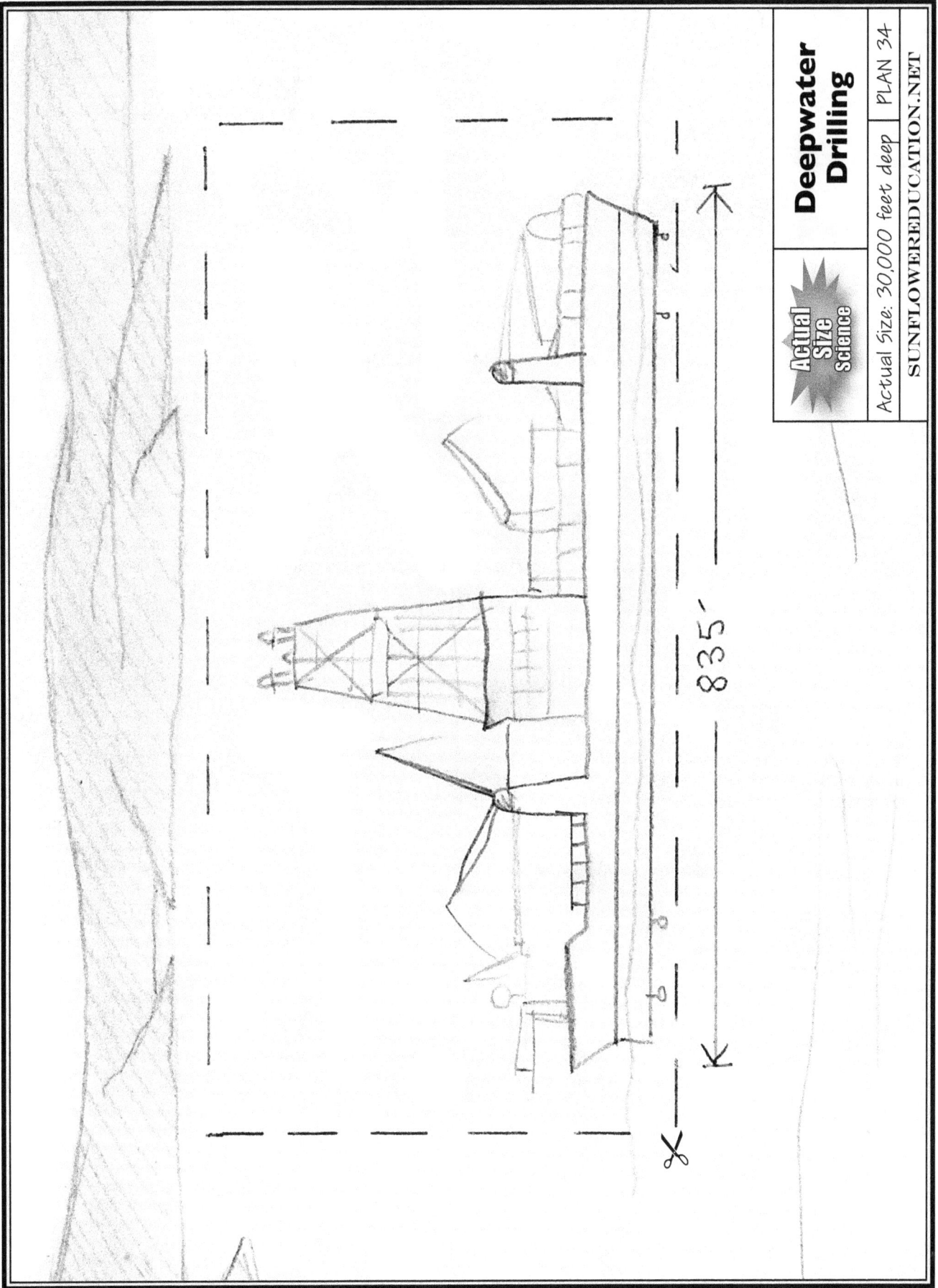

Deepwater Drilling

Actual Size Science

Actual Size: 30,000 feet deep | PLAN 34

SUNFLOWEREDUCATION.NET

835'

Longest Train

Students create a scale model of the world's largest train in order to visualize its amazing length.

Prepare

- *Allow time:* approximately 1 hour for this activity
- *Gather materials:* Plan 35, measuring stick or measuring wheel, sidewalk chalk, tape or glue, scale locomotives and train cars

Focus

Ask students to guess where they might find the world's longest trains. Then tell them that they would be found in Mauritania, a country in Western Africa. These trains run between iron mines in one part of the country to a *port*, Nouadhibou in another. The trains can be up to 1.6 miles long!

Present

❶ Consult Plan 35. Make three photocopies of the Plan. Cut out the *locomotive* and two cars from each one. On the playground (or appropriate indoor floor), draw a line that is 100 feet long, or simply place a mark at 100 feet. Using tape or glue, put the three locomotives together and attach 3 of the cars. Put the remaining three cars together and place them at the end of the 100-foot line. Ask students to imagine that the whole line is filled with cars. This should give them an idea of how long these trains can be. Be sure to point out the passengers hitching rides. (Note: the model train is HO scale.)

❷ Explain to students that on the Mauritania Railway, trains are pulled by three or four locomotives. These locomotives pull the whole train behind them, which is made up of more than 200 cars!

❸ Each car can carry up to 84 tons of *iron ore*. Explain to students that a ton weighs 2,000 pounds. If a ton weighs 2,000 lbs., how much do 84 tons weigh? Have students work together to answer the question, using chalk to make the calculations. The answer is 168,000 lbs. That's a lot of iron! Explain that iron is used largely to make steel. What things in their world are made of steel?

—————————————— *Vocabulary* ——————————————

port: a harbor where ships load and unload before they sail to other countries to trade
locomotive: a powered rail vehicle used for pulling train cars
iron ore: a rock or mineral in which iron can be found

Conclude

So what is iron anyway, and why is it important? Iron is a strong metal, used in everything from the pots and pans in your kitchen to the bridges that cars drive over. The trains in Mauritania transport iron ore, or rocks and minerals in which iron can be found.

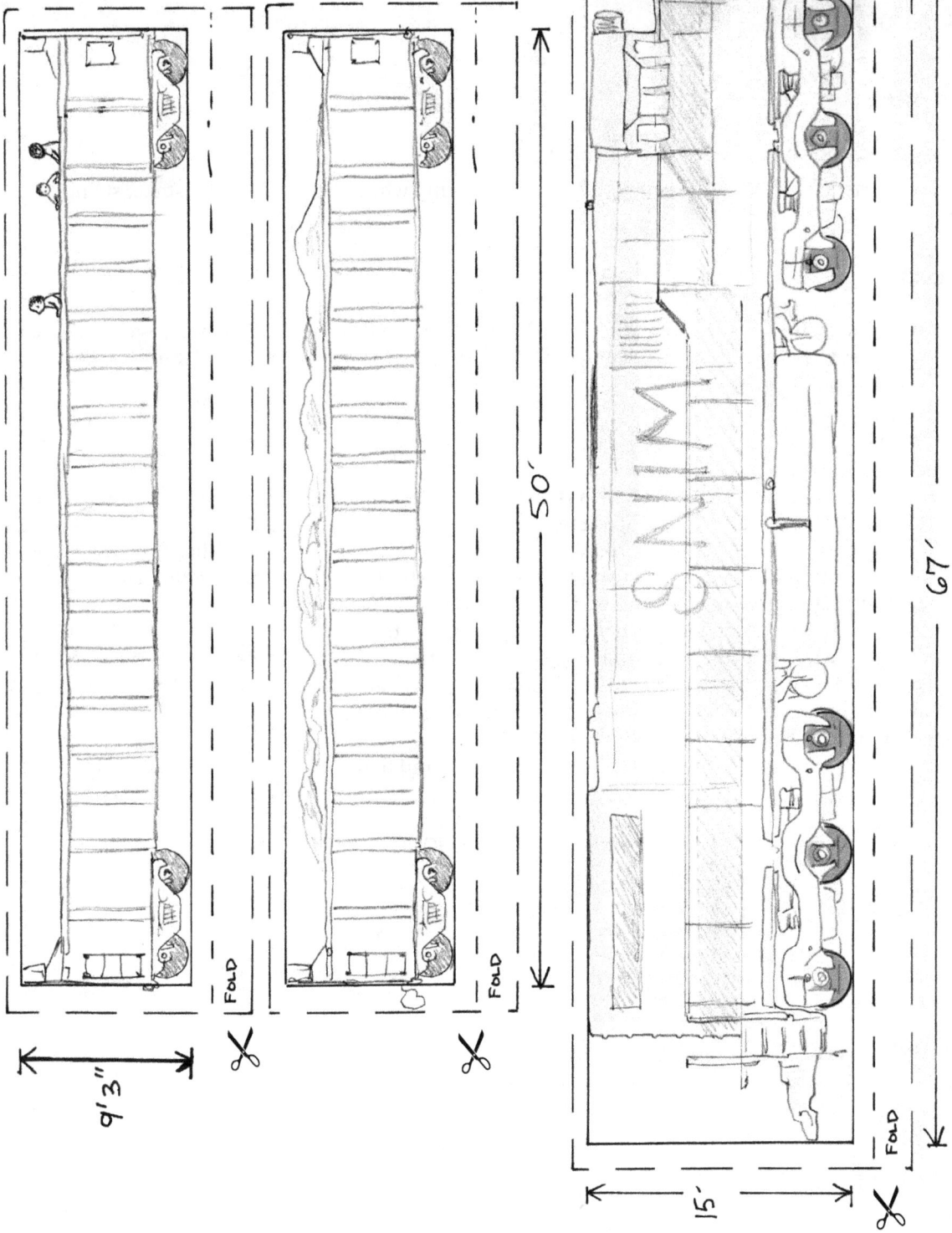

Actual Size Science

Longest Train

Actual Size: 1.6 miles long | PLAN 35

SUNFLOWEREDUCATION.NET

9'3"

50'

FOLD

FOLD

67'

15'

FOLD

SPARWOOD B.C.

Activity 36
Largest Truck
Students create an actual-sized outline of the world's largest truck in order to appreciate its size.

Prepare

- *Allow time:* approximately 1 hour for this activity
- *Gather materials:* Plan 36, measuring stick or measuring wheel, sidewalk chalk, stake, string

Focus

If you like trucks, then you will love the TEREX. Don't worry, though—it's not a dinosaur, but a truck used in the *mining* industry. It is 26 feet tall, 51 feet long, and it can carry a *lot* of stuff!

Present

1 Consult Plan 36. On the playground (or appropriate indoor floor), draw a line that is 51 feet and 1 inch long. Draw another, 26-foot line at a right angle to the first line. Complete the rectangle. Now draw the wheels. From the bottom left-hand corner, measure out 13 feet and 10 inches. This is where you should draw the first wheel, which is 13 feet 6 inches in diameter. Place a stake in the ground and tie a 6' 8" piece of string to it (or have a student stand in one place and hold the string). Hold the end of the string and, keeping the string taught, draw a circle as you walk around the stake in the middle. From the bottom right-hand corner, measure out 15 feet and 5 inches.

Draw the second wheel here in the same way you drew the first. Using Plan 36 as a guide, complete the rest of the truck.

2 This truck can haul up to 400 *tons!* That is 800,000 pounds. Compare this to the average seven-year-old, who weighs 50 lbs.

─────────────── Vocabulary ───────────────

mining: the process of obtaining metals and stones from the ground

ton: 2,000 pounds

Conclude

The TEREX has been renamed as the Bucyrus MT6300AC. If students had the chance to name the world's largest truck, what would they name it? Encourage creative responses.

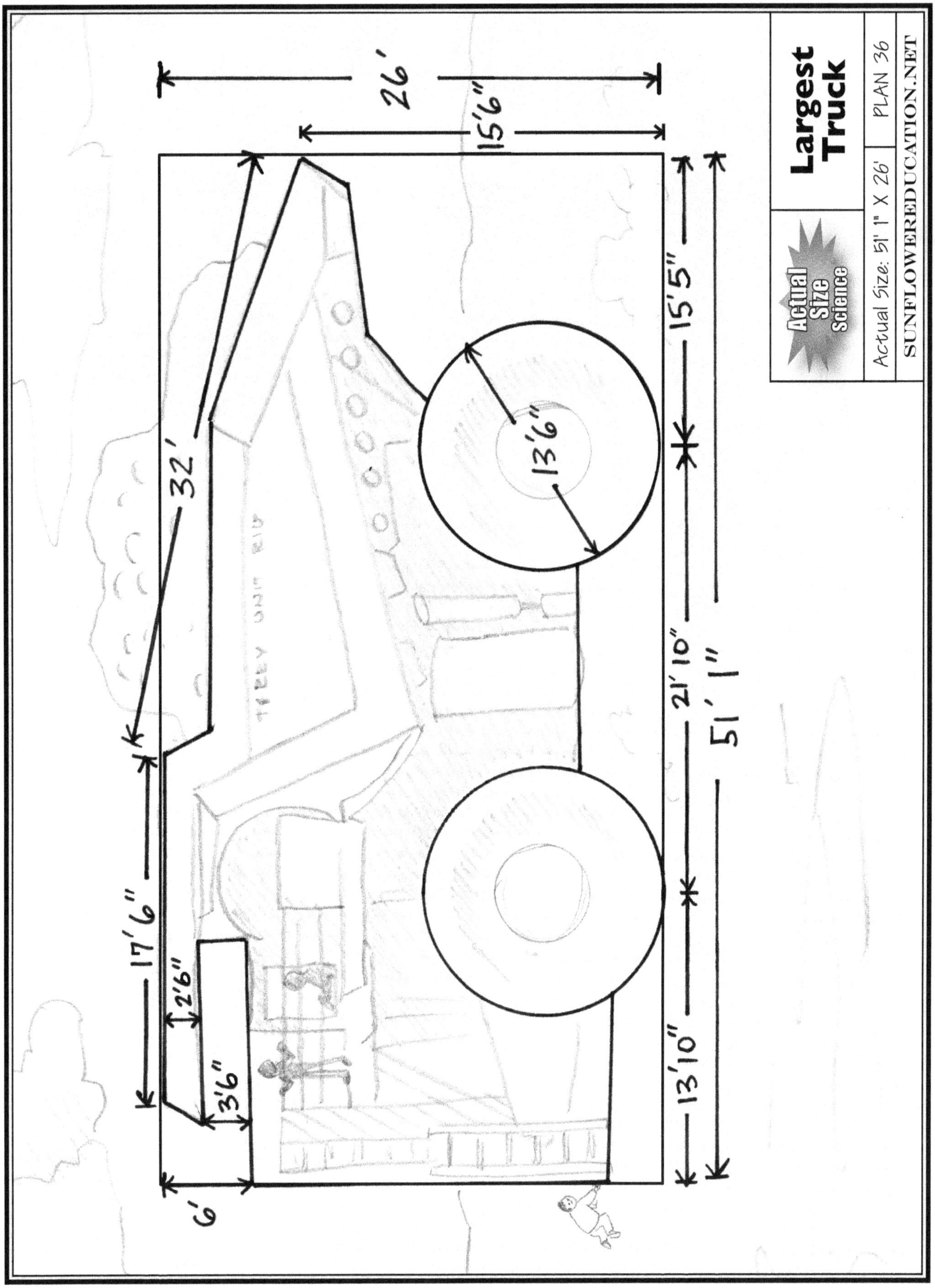

26'

15'6"

15'5"

13'6"

21'10"

51' 1"

13'10"

32'

17'6"

2'6"

3'6"

6'

Largest Truck

Actual Size: 51' 1" X 26'   PLAN 36

Actual Size Science

SUNFLOWEREDUCATION.NET

www.ingramcontent.com/pod-product-compliance
Lightning Source LLC
Chambersburg PA
CBHW081237090426

42738CB00016B/3332